Tracking Your School's Success

Tracking Your School's Success:

A Guide to Sensible Evaluation

☐ Joan L. Herman

☐ Lynn Winters

CORWIN PRESS, INC.
A Sage Publications Company
Newbury Park, California

This work was developed at the Center for Research on Evaluation, Standards, and Student Testing, Center for the Study of Evaluation, Graduate School of Education, University of California, Los Angeles.

The research reported herein was conducted with partial support from the U.S. Department of Education, Office of Educational Research and Improvement, pursuant to Grant No, G00869003. However, the opinions expressed do not necessarily reflect the position or policy of this agency, and no official endorsement by the agency should be inferred.

This work is published and distributed by Corwin Press, Inc., Newbury Park, California, under an exclusive agreement with The Regents of the University of California.

For information address:

Corwin Press, Inc.
A Sage Publications Company
2455 Teller Road
Newbury Park, California 91320

SAGE Publications Ltd.
6 Bonhill Street
London EC2A 4PU
United Kingdom

SAGE Publications India Pvt. Ltd.
M-32 Market
Greater Kailash I
New Delhi 110 048 India

Printed in the United States of America

Library of Congress Cataloging-in-Publication Data

Herman, Joan L.
Tracking your school's success: a guide to sensible evaluation / Joan L. Herman, Lynn Winters.
p. cm.
Includes bibliographical references (p.) and index.
ISBN 0-8039-6024-7
1. Educational evaluation—United States. 2. School management and organization—United States—Decision-making. I. Winters, Lynn. II. Title.
LB2822.75.H47 1992 92-3695
379.1'54—dc20 CIP

01 02 03 10 9 8 7

Corwin Press Production Editor: Tara S. Mead

Contents

Acknowledgments

This book is the product of a multi-year research project conducted by the Center for Research on Evaluation, Standards, and Student Testing (CRESST) with funding from the United States Department of Education, Office of Education Research and Improvement. Our project would not have been possible without the contributions and cooperation of many individuals and organizations. We gratefully acknowledge their help and support.

Teachers and administrators in schools across the country who pilot-tested the evaluation model.

School board members, superintendents, and principals throughout California who participated in our research on evaluation utility and reporting issues.

Members of the California School Boards Association and the Association of California School Administrators who provided valuable review of early versions.

Colleagues in Division H of the American Education Research Association who critiqued our initial concept and provided needed encouragement, with particular thanks for support and suggestions from Carol Robinson, Todd Endo, Sandy Williams, Stella Port, Mardell Kolls, Tom Mann, and Dick Jaeger.

Special thanks to Covina Valley School District, Jack Rankin, Superintendent, for the use of their model school report cards. At CRESST/UCLA, we are grateful to Eva Baker, CRESST co-director, for her conceptualization of sensible evaluation which undergirds the our work. Our sincere thanks also to Shari Golan who directed the library research and coordinated the day-to-day operations; and to Judy Miyoshi and Melissa Goldberg who provided excellent administrative and secretarial support.

Finally, we would like to thank the following friends and family for the intellectual, emotional, and sensible support they provided for this project:

Michelle Herman, Joel Muñoz, and Karla Winters

About the Authors

Joan L. Herman is Associate Director of the UCLA Center for the Study of Evaluation and its Center for Research on Evaluation, Standards, and Student Testing. A former elementary teacher and current Chair of the Board of Education at Stephen S. Wise School, her research interests focus on the use of evaluation and testing to improve schools, the development of multipurpose school-based evaluation systems, and the effects of technology in schools. She has been active in teacher training, recently in the area of developing alternative assessments of student performance, and is widely experienced in program evaluation at all levels. She is editor of the popular second edition of the *Program Evaluation Kit* and primary author of its *Evaluator's Handbook*. Other recent books include *Making Schools Work for Underachieving Minority Students*.

Lynn Winters is Assessment Director of the Galef Institute, a non-profit educational organization dedicated to serving at-risk students through arts-based curricular and instructional interventions. She currently is directing the development of performance and portfolio assessments for a K-6 arts-infused social studies curriculum. She has more than 15 years experience in school-level evaluation as both a research director and a consultant since leaving the high school classroom. She is also Lecturer in Social Research Methods for the UCLA Graduate School of Education. Active in the Program Evaluation division of the American Educational Research Association, she serves as a reviewer for the journal *Educational Evaluation and Policy Planning*.

Introduction

Evaluation—A Management Tool

New Demands on the Schools

The demand for increased productivity.

We educators are living in a time of decreasing resources and increasing demands both from the communities we serve and from the wider body politic. Our morning newspaper regularly reproaches us about the declining quality of American education, the unfavorable standing of American students on international assessments in mathematics and science, and the poor productivity of our schools. Each baleful article includes test scores and statistics to bolster its incontrovertible assertions. State legislatures, in an attempt to finance increasing public needs with shrinking revenues, exhort us to become more productive and accountable and legislate solutions such as "choice," "restructuring," or "school-based management" as ways to leverage the educational dollar. It is no wonder that those of us still optimistic enough to seek out the challenges of educational leadership ask ourselves with each new school improvement initiative, "Don't I already have enough to do?"

The answer: Yes! And the solution for those of us implementing new accountability, restructuring, and improvement mandates who wish to remain sane is to do with our time what legislators would have us do with their monies—get more "bang for the buck." In industry, increasing productivity generally means producing a larger quantity of goods and services using the same amount of resources. In education, productivity is not so easily defined. Increasing our productivity implies improving the quality of our processes and outcomes while tailoring our services to an increasing number of specialized clients (including limited English speaking, physically or educationally handicapped, developmentally delayed, and children of working parents). Unlike industry, our business is people intensive; changes are mediated by the attitudes and skills of our staffs. Educational productivity cannot simply be mandated; nor can we be mechanized. Teaching machines, film projectors, and computers (for the most part) have not changed the way our classrooms look and operate. On the other hand, powerful ideas and research-based instructional strategies such as cooperative/collaborative learning, process-based writing instruction, and meaning-centered mathematics instruction have. For those of us who already have more than enough to do, doing more with even less is only possible if we acquire new techniques that allow us to leverage our already limited time into strategies for meeting new mandates and challenges.

Help for the beleaguered.

Tracking Your School's Success: A Guide to Sensible Evaluation is designed to increase your productivity by presenting some simple, yet powerful techniques for looking at your school and making decisions that will address its most immediate problems. Tracking your success is simply tracking your *progress.* This book provides techniques for tracking where you are going, monitoring where you are, and identifying strategies for getting you where you want to be. Tracking your success means using evaluation as a tool for implementing changes from school-based management, to a better accountability system, to complete restructuring. Tracking your success also means that, by using evaluation techniques to monitor your school, each year's agenda will be more focused and the basis for your decision making clearer (and fairer) to all in your school community. You will know how your efforts relate to school outcomes and will be able to use this information to create a sensible plan for school improvement.

Why Evaluate?

A switch from informal to formal decision making.

School-based management and restructuring, by placing more authority and responsibility at the school level, shift accountability from the district to the site. Suddenly, constituencies who used to be referred "downtown" for information must be addressed by site managers and staff. This shift in accountability forces school staff to formalize and make public both their decision-making processes and the information upon which their decisions are based. Local evaluation is a powerful tool that supports this process.

The challenge is for educators to configure evaluation strategies sensitive to the unique needs and priorities of individual schools—strategies that will inform the goals educators are trying to achieve and the processes they are endeavoring to implement that, at the same time, will be credible to ever more skeptical audiences. The opportunity lies in the fact that school-based management and school restructuring place authority in the hands of those who have always been held accountable for educational outcomes: teachers and principals. When both power and responsibility reside in the same institution, a unique climate is created, one in which evaluation and assessment efforts can actually stimulate school improvement.

Small change, large payoff.

The new demand for schools to adopt an explicit and documented decision-making process can yield unexpected returns. First, a formal, public system of tracking your progress can assure parents that their chosen school is dedicated to meeting the needs of their children. The school community widens each year and the public's appetite for information seems to be growing. School-level progress tracking has even been mandated in some states. In California, for example, legislation guaranteeing minimal levels of school funding requires all schools to issue an annual accountability "report card" to any and all interested people at least once a year. Among the areas covered by such report cards are the following:

- curriculum
- instruction
- parent-community relations
- school climate
- staffing
- student outcomes

For schools operating under similar accountability mandates, the report card can provide a starting point for school-level evaluation and program improvement. Customized to your school's unique goals, such report cards can be a powerful strategy for heralding your successes. Table I.1 provides an example of a report card for a high school. Resource E has examples of report cards for an elementary school and a middle school.

Relevance.

Second, evaluation conducted at the school level can improve the quality of information used to make management, program, and instructional decisions. Who among us has not wondered what effect the implementation of whole language, literature-based language arts instruction or the elimination of "selective" criteria for entrance into advanced placement classes would have on politically important indicators such as state test scores or college admission? A formal, or more explicit, evaluation process provides information about new programs and practices that are credible to both advocates and skeptics.

TABLE I.1 Excerpt From Coastal Village High School Report Card, May 1991

School Profile

Founded in 1955, Coastal Village serves 3,150 students in grades 9-12. Our cosmopolitan student body represents over 40 languages and cultures. Currently, 17% of our students are classified as limited English proficient. Our ethnic mix is 25% Hispanic, 18% Asian, 7% African American, 10% Pacific Islander, and 40% white. We have 20% of our student body enrolled in gifted education programs and 16% served by special education.

Staff

Of our 75 teachers, over 50% have master's degrees and two hold doctorates. Our specialized staff includes a librarian, nurse, activities director, athletic director, four counselors, and a computer specialist. Administration includes a principal and three assistants, one each in charge of counseling, curriculum, and discipline/athletics.

Professional development activities included six teachers attending the national mathematics teachers' conference; two, the social studies; and eight, the English. The county provided training in collaborative learning, integrating social studies and the arts, and peformance assessment. We also had required training in CPR, child abuse reporting, and earthquake preparedness.

Curriculum and Instruction

Students are required to take six classes and need 250 credits to graduate. Social studies and English are required for four years, mathematics and science for three. The elective program is extensive and features a robotics program and an arts "school within a school." This year, we are offering Japanese and Russian, statistics, and sculpture for the first time as a result of student interest. A second innovation is the substitution of an integrated English-social studies-art history humanities core in place of the traditional two periods of English and history. Other curriculum changes include the elimination of "tracked" classes and screening tests for advanced placement classes.

Student Outcomes

About 40% of our seniors take the SAT. Scores for the past year were Verbal, 472, and Math, 501. There were no large differences in performance between boys and girls. About 70% of our students enroll in higher education: 15% at the state university, 25% at state colleges, and 30% at two-year institutions. About 7% join the military. The average freshman GPA for our students attending universities is 2.7; it is 2.9 for those in community colleges.

Attendance averages 85% with February being the month with poorest attendance. Our dropout rate is 4%, evenly distributed among Hispanics, whites, and Pacific Islanders.

Last year five students won National Merit Scholarships, four won art or music contests, two were finalists in the National Geography Bee, and our Math Team came in third in the state.

TABLE I.1 Continued

School Climate

Students are expected to maintain appropriate behavior and sign the honor code each September. Violations result in detention. We provide many opportunities for student recognition, which include the Trip to Washington for Good Citizenship, Student of the Month, Principal's Honor Roll, student government, performing arts ensembles, and intramural athletics.

Parent Involvement

Senior citizens donate over 100 hours a week as classroom aides, and parents have raised nearly $2,000 through Booster Clubs and magazine drives to fund our annual court house visit and Washington trips. Parent volunteers serve as translators during LEP screening and in sheltered classrooms on an as-needed basis.

Budget

We receive $3,231 per student in state funding, which is supplemented by student fees for parking, athletics, and materials as well as parent gifts (totaling over $7,500 last year). The average teacher salary is $34,000 (about 83% of the budget) and the principal earns $60,000. Administrative costs are 8.3% of the budget.

When we have limited resources, decisions about which programs are worthwhile require more stringent criteria than "the kids like it" or "teachers say it's a great program." We are also operating in a climate of public dissatisfaction with the schools in general (though polls show parents feel their own schools are exemplary). Thus new programs are nearly always instituted with less than full support. Parents welcome change but not change that makes school *different* than those they remember: Where are those worksheets? Why is my child playing with beans, blocks, and an abacus instead of learning the times tables? How can my child possibly write without being able to identify gerunds? Information about program outcomes can calm these concerns or help you improve newly adopted curriculum to incorporate the benefits of former approaches into current ones.

Timeliness. Third, school-level evaluation activities provide parents, teachers, principals, and even district administrators with concrete evidence of school improvement or quality in a timely manner. Data gathered at the site, unlike data gathered during district or state assessment and evaluation programs, are manageable in quantity, generally easily understood (they are not subject to the esoteric transformations characteristic of large-scale testing programs), related to local questions and concerns, and summarizable in a reasonable period of time. Timeliness and relevance are perhaps two of the best reasons for engaging in local evaluation.

Broadens the school's perspective.

Finally, school-based evaluation reinforces a school-wide vision. A parent's primary concern is with what happens to the child. A teacher's foremost concern often is with the group of children being taught. Evaluation provides a framework for engaging teachers, parents, and the wider school community in the improvement process as well as a mechanism for informing all involved of school successes and strengths. This larger perspective helps build support for the local school as well as increased mutual understanding among different members of the school community.

What Is School-Based Evaluation?

Tracking your success.

School people—principals, counselors, program coordinators, teachers, and aides—are constant, often unconscious, evaluators. In the course of their daily work, school staff make decisions based on informal data-gathering strategies and then assess the adequacy of those decisions with further data, both formal and informal.

- Principals use district-level enrollment projections, informal reports from teachers, and inquiries from parents to determine staffing and classroom assignments for the next school year.
- School and district administrators plan staff development programs based on needs ascertained through observing informal classroom activities, monitoring new educational trends, and determining whether local school conditions are appropriate for trying innovations as well as listening to teacher concerns in the faculty room.
- Administrators and teachers carefully monitor standardized test scores to see whether schools are "measuring up" and to determine whether any problems are surfacing in the instructional program.
- Teachers and principals use Back-to-School and parent nights for feedback about parent concerns.
- Many high schools track their success by monitoring what happens to graduates (and those who don't graduate) and how students stack up on such indicators as number of academic courses taken, college freshman GPA, and number of students with chronic absence problems.
- Administrators often compare their schools with others they deem similar by using such common measures as number of awards received, years of accreditation granted, special grants

received, Academic Decathlon performance, test scores, and, of course, athletic record.

Those of us who are teaching or who have taught are adept "progress trackers." We become "kid watchers," gathering data about student attitudes and preferences, classroom performance, written and oral performance, and formal grades on quizzes, tests, and projects. We use this as a basis for making a range of classroom management decisions:

- Which lessons are appropriate for which groups of students? What skills should be covered? How much and what kinds of instruction and practice are needed?
- How should students be assigned to groups for instruction? For practice? How often should groups be changed?
- Why is a particular student not doing well? What would help? How can I challenge a particular student and keep interest high?
- How are my students doing? Compared with last year's group? Compared with other classes? Compared with grade-level progress criteria?
- Do my students know what they're supposed to know about this unit? Have they acquired the skills/concepts specified in the course of study? Do they know it "well enough"?
- What kinds of lessons/activities will help students who are not meeting standards to improve? Who should be involved in helping students, parents, aides?
- How can I do a better job? Why did today's lesson bomb? How can I provide more useful comments on student papers? What would make this lesson more relevant to students? What kinds of activities would make the lesson concepts easier to understand?

It's a simple transition to move from classroom to school-level evaluation. Substitute the word "program" for "classroom," and "school" for "student," and you will have identified some questions that are central to school improvement.

In a nutshell, regardless of level, much of our routine progress tracking is designed to answer two simple questions:

- How are we doing?
- How can we improve?

If we add to these two questions an equally important query, "How can we share our successes?" we have captured the purpose of school-based evaluation. We all bring to this school-level evaluation process much experience in gathering information that will help us do our jobs better.

What Are the Pitfalls in Evaluation?

Although school-based evaluation is a powerful management technique, a warning to potential users is in order. Evaluation has strong potential utility, but its promise has generally exceeded its delivery. Evaluation, especially in schools, has too often been identified as "testing." Although test data may be useful in tracking your progress, to define evaluation narrowly as testing can limit the utility of an evaluation. Often imposed from the top down, standardized tests are seen by many outside of the schools as the key measure of educational quality. Tests have been used to satisfy legislators and administrators at the federal, state, and even local levels who wished to know how mandated and other special programs were working and whether schools were effective. Until recently, school people—teachers and administrators—have been viewed primarily as data providers rather than data users and as implementors of reforms rather than initiators of such efforts.

Limitations of standardized tests.

Teachers and local program designers, meanwhile, have raised serious questions about the validity of these top-down assessments, arguing that required tests often are not well matched to their program goals, do not reflect their instructional techniques, and are inappropriate for particular groups of students (Herman, 1990; Herman & Dorr-Bremme, 1983). These critics have been joined by prominent researchers who also have questioned the value of standardized tests for such a broad range of purposes (Eisner, 1985; Sirotnik & Burstein, 1985). The most widely cited critics of current testing practice assert that standardized tests

- provide a very limited view of educational quality;
- examine only a narrow slice of the curriculum;
- emphasize basic skills at the expense of higher-order reasoning or content learning; and
- ignore the multiplicity of academic, social, and vocational goals that schools are supposed to address.

Furthermore, there have been serious questions about what standardized test scores really mean (Cannell, 1987; Linn, Graue, & Sanders, 1990). Do increased scores denote improved achievement or do they reflect a narrowing of the curriculum and teaching to the test? Do high test scores indicate that students can indeed read adequately, write well, and solve problems involving mathematics in real-life settings? In short, the utility of current measures of student achievement for judging educational quality may be severely limited.

Testing is not evaluation.

But, even if better tests were available, more broadly based tests administered, and the results more sensitive to local social and community contexts, *testing* would not be synonymous with *evaluation.* Test scores, or any other single piece of information, provide only a partial picture of school quality and are incomplete for the purposes of educational planning and school decision making. Tests cannot provide full answers to such important questions as:

- Why are outcomes as they are?
- Which parts of the school program are working well? Which are not?
- Which students are benefiting most? Who needs more attention?

Understanding the processes that create or contribute to school outcomes and the contexts in which these relationships occur is a prerequisite for developing a program improvement agenda.

Evaluation is not limited to comparing programs or schools.

Just as the reliance on test scores alone provides a narrow view of the evaluation process, engaging in evaluation activities only for the purpose of deciding which program or school is "better" gives short shrift to the wide range of purposes to which evaluation is suited. At the school level, where curriculum goals may be decided by an outside agency and where decisions about whether to retain or replace a program can be dependent upon a state textbook adoption cycle or system-wide change, evaluating a program to "see if it's any good" often is not an option. Rather, the focus is on "how can we improve what we're doing?" Similarly, school-level program decisions center on identifying needs, setting school site or program priorities, and tracking progress both in implementing change and in student outcomes. Although large-scale federal and state evaluations still focus on judgments of worth and comparisons of programs, more current evaluation theories emphasize the role of data-gathering activities to aide decision making and build support for institutions and programs (Alkin, 1985; Patton, 1988).

Data don't solve problems.

Those of us old enough to remember Skinner boxes, teaching machines, the age of video, and management by objectives have learned that a technique or technology cannot transform a school. The power of evaluation does not lie solely in its "scientific" methods or "hard" data (numbers). We know they're hard because we have to crunch them prior to digesting them. Evaluation information alone cannot solve problems; only thoughtful and empowered educators will solve problems. The power of evaluation rests in its ability to help people identify where they are going, how to improve the journey, and whether they have arrived. It is a process for communicating, building support, and developing a shared vision among the school community.

A Better Approach: School-Based Evaluation

The litany of problems in current evaluation practice contains the roots of a more productive, sensible model, one that better supports restructuring and school-based decision making. What are the features of sensible, school-based evaluation?

Sensible evaluation.

Sensible evaluation is *formulated in collaboration* with program administrators and implementors. Sensible evaluation is *useful;* useful evaluations are designed with input from both those who know the program best as well as those who are responsible for improving the program.

Sensible evaluation is *well aligned* with school goals and priorities. It matches tools and assessments with what the school or program is trying to accomplish. Sensible evaluation focuses on what school people agree are important goals.

Sensible evaluation, while maximally responsive to the needs and concerns of the school, is at least minimally *responsive to the accountability and monitoring concerns* of the local district and state. Sensible evaluation provides information on general indicators while documenting progress on specific local goals.

Sensible evaluation focuses on the *theories guiding program actions as well as the short- and long-term targets of change.* Educational programs are based on theories, often implicit, that guide program development. These theories define what actions are required to improve education for children, and they predict that, if certain activities occur, certain outcomes can be expected. Sensible evaluation focuses both on the current theory-based actions as well as on the predicted outcomes. For example, one school might be interested in exploring the effects on student language acquisition of implementing a whole language approach to literacy instruction. The ultimate target, of course, is student language performance, a target that realistically may not be dramatically affected for several years. The short-term view, however, can focus on what needs to happen in the meantime: comprehensive staff development, acquisition of new materials, practice in implementing new techniques, parent education. Evaluation needs to attend to the critical features of the theory of action underlying the whole language program so that progress can be monitored over both the short and the long term.

Sensible evaluation, though guided by theories of action, is attentive to *unanticipated side effects.* Although we focus on implementing certain theory-based strategies hoping to accomplish intended goals, we need to be sure that we're not falling behind or causing havoc with other school outcomes. If, for example, we are focusing on the effects a program is having in raising student achievement, we might want to check that these gains are not coming at the expense of student attitudes or even attrition. Or, in another example, if a small group of teachers is involved in a project, are there negative side effects in their relations with the rest of the faculty? Negative side effects indicate areas needing attention. Positive side effects add evidence of the success of the program.

Sensible evaluation designs encompass a *variety of indicators* of school quality and student accomplishments. *Multiple measures triangulate on a variety of important outcomes.* Schooling is a complex process with complex outcomes; its quality cannot be captured by a single score on a single test given on a single occasion. Sensible evaluations include a variety of measures that assess

- a range of outcomes;
- important dimensions of school, program, and instructional processes; and
- key aspects of school context and demographics.

Sensible evaluation uses *measures yielding valid inferences about* programs, processes, and outcomes. The validity of currently available measures for school decision making is only approximate, with some current measures more open to question than others. One step toward improving our decisions about schools is to use measures aligned with the critical features of the local school context, processes, and outcomes. A second safeguard against the imperfection of our current tests is the use of multiple measures to *replicate* findings of school effects so that we can be more confident about what has occurred.

Sensible evaluation concentrates on doing *a few things well* using as much *existing information* as possible. Schools are busy places that happen to produce a lot of information as by-products of the kind of work school people do. Building upon existing information minimizes the burden of data collection and maximizes the usefulness of currently mandated school records and information archives.

Sensible evaluators know that certain kinds of evaluation activities provide staff both with *insights about curriculum* and with *new skills.* A prominent example of an evaluation activity that has a large staff-development payoff is scoring of performance assessments. In the process of reviewing student work and refining or developing criteria for rating, staff come to better understand the theories underlying and predicting student performance.

Sensible evaluation examines *progress over time.* Because measurement in education, as in most fields, is inexact and subject to error as well as to influences from a variety of factors, and because programs are not implemented under pristine conditions, conclusions based on one point in time are unlikely to be reliable. Judgments of success about innovations are more credible when the analysis provides trends for several years both before and after an innovation is implemented. Use of an extended time frame for making decisions about schools is also a response to the reality that change is slow; it takes time to get new approaches up and running and producing results.

Sensible evaluation has *explanatory power.* When an evaluation includes information about school and community contexts and on processes as well as outcomes, we can examine the interrelationships among these to understand why things are as they are. Without an understanding of these interrelationships, evaluations cannot really answer the question of why a program is working well or what actions should be taken to improve it.

When to Track Your Progress With Evaluation

Because evaluation requires administrator and staff time, the scarcest commodity in schools, you should carefully select the decision areas to be informed by it. Although no general principle exists that can tell you: "you need to do an evaluation in this circumstance," the questions below will help you identify the decision contexts where formal evaluation processes are routinely used:

- Is this a high-stake decision? Will many students or teachers be affected by the outcome of the actions to be taken?
- Do I need highly credible or even legally defensible information to support this decision?
- Do we need to know how a program works and why it produces the effects it does?
- Is my funding contingent on providing information to describe a program or its effectiveness?

Involve Others and Increase Your Power

While you are considering whether evaluation is appropriate, you should identify potential "stakeholders" for your evaluation—those groups expected to act on findings and others likely to be affected by or interested in your results. Stakeholder groups may include teachers, administrators (site, district, or state), parents, students, board members, or specific community constituencies such as the business roundtable, civic groups, social service providers, or realtors. It is important to involve stakeholder groups early and often in the evaluation process. Their involvement will help to build consensus, or at least common understanding for negotiation, about decisions based on evaluation finding. Involvement of stakeholders will promote the credibility of findings and will increase the likelihood that findings will indeed influence action. Stakeholder involvement not only increases ownership in decisions influenced by the evaluation but also increases the pool of available help in focusing the evaluation, defining its guiding questions, gathering information, and understanding results. In other words, consider early who your most important stakeholders are and consider convening their representatives in an ongoing advisory group for your evaluation efforts.

Tracking Your Success in Six Steps

Once you are satisfied that you need an evaluation and you have identified relevant stakeholder groups, you are ready to implement the six-step decision-making process we call "evaluation." Although others have suggested a different number of steps, our model shares with many evaluation models a number of common features:

- a process for clarifying the actual decisions or actions to be taken as well as the questions, issues, or goals of the evaluation activity;
- a reliance on multiple sources of information for decision making;
- an externally verifiable decision-making process; and
- a belief that data will indeed result in better decisions about schools.

Steps in the evaluation process are neither linear nor fixed. Some steps may be taken simultaneously, and there is often an interplay between steps, with information from one step changing activities or decisions made at another. Like all problem-solving strategies, the evaluation process is recursive. An insight gained in one step might cause rethinking of the evaluation questions or a revision in data gathering instruments. A review of results may shift the focus of the evaluation or suggest additional or more important questions. And data collection, analysis, and reporting may occur over a very short time period so as to appear almost simultaneous.

In our work at CRESST (the UCLA Center for Research on Evaluation, Standards, and Student Testing), we have found the following steps to be useful in guiding our evaluation activities:

(1) *Focus the evaluation.* Determine the purpose(s) of the evaluation: the decisions to be made, the possible audiences or people affected by these decisions, and the questions we might ask that would enlighten our decisions.

(2) *Identify tracking strategies.* Determine what information we might need to answer our questions or better understand the consequences of our decisions. Make initial decisions about the kinds of instruments needed. How will information be collected? Will there be interviews? Observations? Focus groups? A review of extant data? Student work samples? Standardized test results?

(3) *Manage instrument development and data collection.* Determine from whom we need information and when. Make a plan

for instrument development if necessary. How long will it take? Who will collect information? What will it cost in time and resources to purchase or develop and administer instruments?

(4) *Score and summarize data.* Think about the kinds of scores you will need to answer your evaluation questions. Choose appropriate scores or scoring strategies if you are using projects, performance tests, or portfolios.

(5) *Analyze and interpret information.* Marshall your score summaries to answer your specific evaluation questions. Work with stakeholders to "make sense" of findings and conclusions in light of shared experiences and possible conflicting interests.

- Look for trends over time to identify strengths and areas for improvement.
- Look for relationships among program processes, student and staff characteristics, and outcomes to explain findings.
- Negotiate a common understanding of findings: make meaning of the trends, profiles, and summaries of questionnaire, test, interview, observation, and/or performance information. Find possible courses of action related to findings.

(6) *Act on findings and continue program monitoring.* Communicate your findings in a timely and appropriate manner. Common methods of communicating findings include school action or school improvement plans, informal meetings, panel discussions, formal presentations, and written reports. Report the results that are useful and clear to your primary stakeholders and other interested audiences. Use different reporting methods to match the audience needs. Develop plans to address school weaknesses and celebrate strengths. Be sure to monitor your plans with—what else?—evaluation.

Table I.2 summarizes the steps in school-based evaluation and highlights the principles of sensible practice.

How to Use This Manual

Tracking Your School's Success is a "user's manual" for school-based evaluation. It is written as a guide for those new to the evaluation process as well as a troubleshooter's manual for those addressing specific program planning, implementation, and accountability concerns. The following chapters present guidelines for conducting each of the six steps and include real-life examples to guide your own evaluation efforts. For those wishing to explore the evaluation process more deeply, Suggested Readings are provided at the end of each section.

TABLE I.2 Principles of Sensible Evaluation

Step	*Sensible Actions*
Focus the Evaluation	Involve significant constituencies Include improvement and accountability concerns Look at long- and short-term targets of change Look at relationships between processes and outcomes based on your theories of action Look for unanticipated side effects
Identify Tracking Strategies	Use strategies well aligned with school goals Use multiple indicators Build in checks for validity of inferences
Manage Instrument Development and Data Collection	Build measures upon existing information Consider accountability mandates Match instruments with specific evaluation questions
Score and Summarize Data	When appropriate, use scoring sessions for staff development Assure valid inferences by choosing appropriate scores
Analyze and Interpret Information	Involve key constituencies Examine progress over time Consider and refine your theories of action Be alert to unanticipated side effects Corroborate findings by using multiple indicators
Act on Findings and Continue Program Monitoring	Use the principles guiding focusing activities to monitor actions based on your findings

Worksheets are provided in Resource D at the end of the book; they have been designed to be used as templates for your own evaluation efforts. You should feel free to reproduce the templates and to modify them to fit your particular situation. Sample versions of the worksheets with possible answers filled in appear in the text.

References

Alkin, M. C. (1985). *A guide for evaluation decision makers.* Beverly Hills, CA: Sage.

Cannell, J. (1987). Nationally normed elementary achievement in America's public schools: How all 50 states are above the national average. *Educational Measurement: Issues and Practice,* 7(4), 12-15.

Eisner, E. (1985). *The art of educational evaluation.* Philadelphia: Falmer.

Herman, J. L. (1990, April). Accountability for testing. *R & D Exchange, 4*(3).

Herman, J. L., & Dorr-Bremme, D. (1983). Achievement testing in American public schools: A national perspective. In E. L. Baker & J. L. Herman (Eds.), *Testing in the nation's schools: Collected papers.* Los Angeles: University of California, Center for the Study of Evaluation.

Linn, R., Graue, M. E., & Sanders, N. M. (1990). *Quality of standard tests: Final report.* Los Angeles: University of California, Center for the Study of Evaluation.

Patton, M. Q. (1988). *Utilization-focused evaluation* (2nd ed.). Newbury Park, CA: Sage.

Sirotnik, K. A., & Burstein, L. (1985). *Making sense out of comprehensive school-based information systems: An exploratory study.* Los Angeles: University of California, Center for the Study of Evaluation.

Suggested Readings

For those wishing more information about evaluation in general or the overall procedures, we offer the following suggestions:

Berk, R. A., & Rossi, P. H. (1990). *Thinking about program evaluation.* Newbury Park, CA: Sage.
Berk introduces the range of questions answered by evaluation and describes methods currently used. Especially helpful are the specific examples of evaluation goals and methods.

Herman, J. L., Morris, L. L., & Fitz-Gibbon, C. T. (1987). *Evaluator's handbook.* Newbury Park, CA: Sage.
The *Handbook* provides step-by-step guidelines for every phase of evaluation from selecting questions to preparing the report. A valuable resource for getting an overview of the nuts and bolts in planning and managing an evaluation. Of particular use is first chapter's synopsis of major evaluation models.

Popham, W. J. (1988). *Educational evaluation* (2nd ed.). Englewood Cliffs, NJ: Prentice-Hall.
Popham's provocative and humorous prose guides the practitioner through evaluation models, writing objectives, measuring achievement and attitudes, evaluation designs, sampling strategies, data analysis, and reporting. It is less specific than the *Handbook* but an almost painless way to learn about the more technical aspects of evaluation.

Rutman, L. (1980). *Planning useful evaluations.* Beverly Hills, CA: Sage.
Do you need to know if your program is evaluable? Before tackling the Augean stables, you may wish to read Rutman's description of factors that affect the evaluability of programs or use his program analysis tools in reviewing your school. Suggestions for enhancing the evaluability of a program are especially helpful.

1

Step One
Focus the Evaluation

Overview

During this first step, you will focus your evaluation by formulating the specific questions you want to address. These identify the specific areas of your school program that will be examined. Plan to convene your advisory board—or other mechanism for involving stakeholders—to assure that the interests of important constituencies are represented.

In the context of school-based management and restructuring, a primary purpose of evaluation is to monitor and improve the quality of school programs or the components of those programs. A second purpose is to provide at least modestly credible data about school progress to district personnel and the public. The simple question, "How are we doing?" perhaps best expresses the focus of school-based evaluation. Deceptively simple and straightforward, yet related to nearly all school functions, the "how are we doing" question subsumes a host of school staff concerns: What student, community, or curricular needs should we be addressing? What should we change in existing programs or what new programs should we adopt to meet these needs? Are we doing well enough? How can we do better? Although "how are we doing?" suggests a concern with "how can we do better?" the question is not limited to examining areas for improvement. Too often, we think of evaluation as an activity to identify school weaknesses when, in fact, it provides ample opportunities for documenting what we do well. All schools have success stories to share and strengths upon which to build.

Focus on Major Program Aspects

Yet, simply asking, "How are we doing?" is not enough to provide a clear evaluation focus. What we should be examining depends upon political and legal requirements, our educational philosophy, and our values. For example, one way to focus our evaluation is to attend to, among other things, what our state or district insists be examined. School accountability report cards, required in a number of states, are one instance of a *mandated focus.* These required areas of reporting can provide a starting point for thinking about important dimensions of school quality. When customized to a school's unique goals and circumstances, such external mandates enable us to highlight our school successes as well to monitor improvement efforts. Furthermore, whether a school improvement effort is sparked by an outside mandate or local initiative, certain aspects of schooling appear time and again as foci of school quality:

- *Student outcomes*: achievement, attitudes, school completion, preparation for work or college
- *Curriculum*: adequacy and effectiveness of educational materials, technology, resources; content coverage; course work requirements; access by different student populations; alignment with state/school goals and assessments
- *Instruction:* strategies, grouping, teacher role, classroom organization, student interaction, use of technology
- *School climate*: consensus on school goals, expectations for student achievement, relationships among and between students and teachers, pride in and satisfaction with school, administrative leadership, teacher empowerment, support for innovation, safety, student and faculty morale
- *Staffing:* staff preparation, professional development, student-staff ratios, staff understanding of student population needs, staff demonstration of special competencies such as being bilingual, understanding mainstreaming techniques or curriculum requirements
- *Parent-community relations:* attendance at school events, parent involvement with child's educational progress, understanding of school goals, support for and value of school, volunteer programs, financial support, business partnerships

Develop a Comprehensive View of School or Program Quality

These aspects of schools are of interest, of course, because many people believe them essential to quality schooling. Although much of public interest centers on student outcomes, those of us in schools know that improvements in student outcomes cannot be accomplished without changes in these other areas. When we look for reasons that outcomes are as they are, as mentioned earlier, we clearly need to look at other aspects of the school environment.

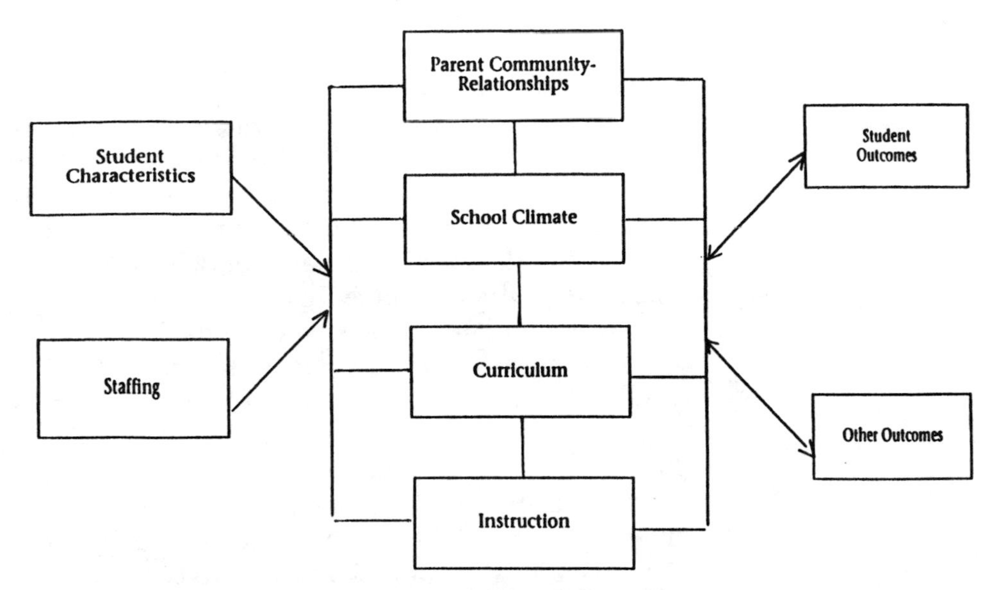

Figure 1.1. A Process Outcome Model of Schooling

And, if we want evaluation to help us to understand how our programs are operating and to clarify underlying reasons for current outcomes, it's helpful to have in mind a model of how these various aspects fit together. Figure 1.1 maps one possible set of relationships between program features and student outcomes. Here we see that student outcomes are thought to be influenced by school and instructional processes of climate, curriculum, and instructional strategies. These in turn are influenced by teacher background and training, parent involvement, and other student and school factors. If student outcomes don't match our goals or expectations, then we need to recycle back through these other areas to identify potential causes and design remedies. Although your "model" may have different features and suppose different sets of relationships, the point is that it is useful to have a broad view of how different aspects of a school fit together.

Each of the areas displayed in Figure 1.1 defines potential areas of focus for an evaluation. At the most general level, we can ask, "How are we doing in student outcomes? In curriculum? In instruction? In school climate?" This is a preliminary step in the focusing process.

Choose a Wide-Angle or Close-Up Perspective

As you identify program area(s) of interest, consider whether you need a broad-spectrum or close-up view of your program. When you are writing a school plan for the first time or deciding upon what might make your school a place that better meets student needs, you will want to look at the big picture. Needs assessment can help give this perspective; it provides the wide-angle shot across the entire school. Like many school report cards, a needs assessment examines the overall quality of school programs and seeks to identify areas of strength and weakness.

In contrast, when you have a specific program you are trying to implement, rather than looking across the whole school, you may want to know how well that program is working and how to improve it. In this instance, you will engage in the process known as *formative evaluation,* looking in greater depth at the operation and effectiveness of specific change efforts.

Both perspectives, either wide angle or close up, address the same general questions: "How are we doing?" "How successful are we?" In needs assessment, we focus broadly on the outcomes of what's happening in our school. In formative evaluation, our emphasis is on how and why it is happening.

An initial task in focusing the evaluation, then, is to decide whether our interests are best served by needs assessment or by formative evaluation. We then must narrow our interests to a manageable number of concerns.

Needs Assessment Questions

As mentioned before, needs assessments are often required steps in program planning and in the school goal setting process. In conducting a needs assessment, we look broadly across all curriculum areas. Having identified an area or two in which we are doing well, we may highlight this with our public or choose to share our successes with other professionals. Certainly, identification of areas of strength is central to the accreditation and school review process. At the same time, we may find an area or two where we have a need to improve. The needs assessment process enables us to look more deeply at these areas in a *diagnostic* sense and to establish some priorities for program planning or revision.

The *needs* in needs assessment most often refers to student needs based on current or past performance data such as standardized test scores, course enrollments, post-high school plans, or language proficiency. State and federal project funding for such projects as Title VII, Chapter 1, or state innovative program grants requires that schools *justify* their need for a particular project by presenting student outcome data pointing to *deficiencies* the project will correct. Parent and staff perceptions, often garnered through beginning or year-end surveys, also are often taken into account.

Although, typically, these mandated project-related needs assessments focus on basic skills achievement data (i.e., reading and mathematics standardized test scores), you need not be so limited. You will want to assess other areas as well, either because they are important problem areas in your school or because they represent a priority for you and/or your important stakeholder groups. Your school might wish to look, for example, at needs in such areas as school climate, parent involvement, instructional quality, use of technology, or school image/public relations.

An important aspect of needs assessment is the identification of the group(s) having the need. If you only examine results for the school as a whole, you may believe that you are "on track." Unfortunately, these overall results may mask significant problems in specific subgroups of students, such as by masking serious performance disparities. Which subgroups might be of interest? You might first look at students participating in special programs, special education, Chapter 1, and bilingual or gifted education. You might pose questions about groups that past experience or research have shown to have special needs. Among these subgroups are students new to a school, working students, girls (in mathematics and science), boys (in writing), or students with erratic attendance. By asking how particular subgroups may be doing, you attend to important equity concerns.

The strategy of asking about specific results for different subgroups also applies to areas other than student outcomes. Different subgroups of parents, teachers, or aides and volunteers might have different insights about the program that could be obscured when data are averaged across the entire population of responses. If you have some notion that different groups might have very different opinions on school operations and/or impact, you should keep these groups in mind. For example, there may be a difference between neighborhood parents and parents of students bussed into a school in their perceptions of how well the new student self-esteem program is working. Or social studies teachers may or may not be observing effects of the new literature-based writing program implemented in the English classes.

Table 1.1 illustrates typical needs assessment questions and may provide a starting point for your own needs assessment efforts.

Formative Evaluation Questions

Formative evaluation questions emerge logically from needs assessment questions. If a group is not performing well in some area or parents are concerned about a program, we institute some change to address the need. As we track our progress in implementing this change, the needs assessment questions that address program aspects remain useful. In particular, we will want to continue to track the needs our change(s) were designed to address.

The path we follow in formative evaluation, however, differs somewhat from that taken for a needs assessment. Although needs assessment questions generally ask us to look at outcomes of one kind or another for specific groups, formative evaluation allows us to look at processes as well. In formative evaluation, we can augment the "how are we doing" question with the more interesting query, "Here's what we're trying to do, what needs to happen to make that a reality?" Most often, what we are trying to do is to make a curricular, organizational,

TABLE 1.1 Typical Needs Assessment Questions

Student Outcomes	After adjusting for changes in test norms or student mobility, in which areas tested by standardized tests have we improved over the last 3 years? Maintained our ranking? Declined?
	Are there performance differences by language proficiency, sex, or ethnicity?
	What are student attitudes toward history, science, math, and/or English? Do attitudes differ by grade level? By particular subgroups of students?
	What is our school completion rate? How does it compare with comparable schools? State averages?
Curriculum	Do we have enough core literature books for each child to take books home?
	Is our curriculum aligned with state frameworks or national curriculum standards? Do we have clear goal statements for each curriculum area?
	Are course goals and expectations comparable for all students regardless of ability or language proficiency?
Instruction	How does our classroom instruction differ from what we consider desirable or optimal practice?
	How is technology used to support instruction and student learning at each grade level?
Staff	What kinds of in-service does staff suggest?
	Do parents and students perceive staff as holding high expectations, being involved with students, and being well prepared?
Parents and Community	Do parents feel comfortable visiting the school? Discussing their child's progress with teachers? Discussing school concerns with administrators?
	Do we provide volunteer opportunities for parents regardless of their educational background, language, or work obligations?
	What community and business partnerships are supporting specific programs and where do we need more support?
School Climate	Is there mutual respect and a positive working relationship among students? Between students and teachers? Between teachers and parents? Between teachers and administrators?
	Do students take pride in their school?
	Do teachers feel supported by administration?
	Is there suppport for change or innovation in this school when such a need exists?
	Do students and teachers feel physically safe at school?

or instructional change that we hope in the long run will improve student outcomes. In the short run, the changes may be aimed at improving the school climate, increasing parent involvement, or changing teaching practices.

Frame your questions in theory of action.

Theories of action are the rationale for why we are using particular programmatic strategies. Theories of action define what essential program features are, how they fit together, and why certain program features are thought to be beneficial for students. For example, if you are trying to change your primary grade curriculum to a whole language approach, your theory of action tells you what the important elements are in that approach and what needs to happen for teachers to change to such an approach. Among the features you would expect to see in a whole language classroom are teachers modeling the reading process by reading aloud to students; students using "real" literature as opposed to basal readers; students engaged in a variety of reading activities from sentence strips to pattern books to student published material; students being asked to reconstruct whole stories, make predictions, identify familiar words; and students writing or talking about their reading. Among the things that might be necessary to encourage teachers to change to such an approach are quality training, follow-up, and availability of appropriate materials.

As you form your evaluation questions, you will want to focus on whether in fact "whole language" is occurring and on whether necessary precursors occurred as well as on the actual reading progress of the students. When you look at programs as *models* of instruction and include questions about processes as well as outcomes, your evaluation results will point out specific ways to improve the program.

By linking your evaluation questions to a larger view of what should be happening in school, you will be able to gather information more directly useful for program improvement. Let's take an example that might occur in any school. During the first year of whole language implementation, student standardized reading test scores drop in some classes but not in others. You find that, because of the way students are assigned, the drop is not attributable to student characteristics. Because you have a theory of action about what whole language instruction is supposed to look like (and produce), you also visited classrooms and noted which aspects teachers were using. In reviewing your observation notes, you find that, in the classes where scores declined, teachers were using more whole language strategies than in classrooms where scores went up. There were no drill and practice or testlike activities. In fact, the only time students encountered a multiple choice format was on the district standardized test. Your theory of action, however, prepared you for this eventuality, so you collected some information related specifically to expected outcomes from a whole language program. Because your action theory suggests that students will be independent readers, you inserted a few questions into your annual parent survey to find out what students read at home and how often they volunteered to read aloud to their parents. You also asked the parents to rate their child's attitude toward reading. Sure enough, parents of students in classrooms where more whole language strategies were used (and where test scores dropped) reported more positive student attitude toward reading and more at-home reading. These data now provide some suggestions for program improvement. You want to maintain positive attitudes yet prevent test scores from dropping drastically. Thus you may wish to have those "further-along" teachers provide at least some practice in test taking while coaching the more traditional teachers in whole language instruction.

Table 1.2 summarizes a few current trends in education. Many of the changes we are implementing in our schools, from whole language instruction, to process-based writing, to meaning-based mathematics, incorporate one or more of these trends. The list may suggest to you what action theory(ies) are related to your own programs and what kinds of questions about program processes you could ask.

Consider the factors underlying successful innovation.

As we are well aware, school improvement is a complex process. The literature on innovation and change in schools suggests that successful change depends upon several concomitant factors (Berman & McLaughlin, 1978):

Teacher consensus about the need for and ownership in the change
Leadership support of the effort
Adequate staff development and follow-up assistance on the implementation specifics
Teacher/staff/school adaptation of the change to meet local needs
Materials and resources required to implement the change

These precursors to successful innovation or change provide areas about which we might ask evaluation questions. They also suggest possible reasons why your programs are or are not working well.

A well-known evaluation model, the Concerns Based Adoption Model (CBAM), was developed specifically to answer evaluation questions related to school-based innovations. Those who wish an in-depth view of this specialized kind of formative evaluation should read the well-written ASCD publication *Taking Charge of Change* (Hord et al., 1987).

Table 1.3 lists typical formative evaluation questions to spark your thinking about your own programs.

TABLE 1.2 Current Trends in Education

Active Learning

The emphasis in both instruction and assessment has shifted from getting students to *respond* to having them *produce or demonstrate* what they know. Meaningful learning is now thought to occur when students have opportunities to tackle real discipline-based problems and interact with the "tools" of the subject. In mathematics, students manipulate concrete objects and derive concepts inductively; they graph, they weigh, they measure, they draw, they write, and they think aloud about real-world problems and how to solve them mathematically using their own strategies. In language arts or literature, students have some choice in what they read and are asked to add their own insights to well-established interpretations. In science, students experiment and manipulate materials instead of reading about experiments or watching demonstrations. Sometimes the experiments are computer simulations, sometimes actual experiments.

Collaborative/Cooperative Learning

In collaborative/cooperative learning, students work in groups on common tasks. Collaboration and cooperation have different manifestations. Most versions advocate heterogeneous grouping. Some versions require that students be graded individually; others require that they receive a group grade.

Contextualized Learning

The impetus for contextualized learning comes from recent research in cognitive psychology, which suggests that "problem solving" or "decision making" or even "reading" have different meanings in different disciplines or contexts. The natural extension of this hypothesis is that skills need to be taught in context. Reading, for example, is really reading about science, literature, social studies, art, mathematics, and so on. Students are asked to apply skills in a variety of contexts under the assumption that the discourse demands change when the context changes. This view calls into question units or courses that emphasize skills apart from subject matter.

Developmentally Appropriate Instruction

Many programs, especially for elementary children, are now founded on developmental learning principles, summarized in Bredenkamp (1987). Developmentally appropriate teaching strategies include an integrated curriculum so that children's learning in all traditional subjects occurs primarily through projects and learning centers that reflect the children's interests and suggestions. The teachers guide children by extending their ideas, responding to their questions, and challenging their thinking. Children are encouraged to evaluate their own work and to understand that errors are a natural and necessary part of learning. Teachers analyze children's errors to plan curriculum and instruction.

continued

TABLE 1.2 Continued

Integrated/Interdisciplinary Instruction

Young children have difficulty separating their world into "subject domains." The separation of learning into "disciplines" is often artificial and ignores the interconnectedness of knowledge. It is now more common to see the elementary curriculum organized around themes or interdisciplinary units that integrate the subject matter of science, social studies, art, and/or music with the skills developed in reading, language arts, and mathematics. At the secondary level, interdisciplinary humanities and math-science programs are becoming more common.

Prior Knowledge as a Basis for Learning

Learning is more efficient and meaningful when students can use what they already know to make connections with new material. Prewriting and prereading activities, where students are asked to recall or brainstorm what they know related to a particular topic, are strategies designed to help students build upon what they know and to refine existing concepts. We recognize that we rarely "start from scratch." Spending time to help students discover or organize what they know related to new learning helps them make connections between prior and new knowledge and helps teachers to plan instruction based on student needs.

Thinking Skills as an Instructional Outcome

Although thinking skills are to be taught in context, transferrable skills, rather than information, are desired outcomes of instruction. The California Frameworks, for example, ask that students develop a range of thinking abilities beyond recall and comprehension. These thinking skills include critical thinking, problem solving, science process knowledge, aesthetic appreciation, and meaning-based communication. The frameworks have as a goal the development of "generic" thinking techniques such as analyzing from multiple perspectives, drawing inferences, and evaluating outcomes.

Authentic Performance Assessment

A trend in classroom testing has been to design tests that look much more like real-life tasks. There is a move to add performance assessments to paper-pencil tests as a way to evaluate student learning. Meaningful assessment is viewed as an integral part of instruction and not separate from it. Meaningful assessment asks students to demonstrate, produce, reflect, and self-evaluate. Assessment is now concerned with diagnosis as well as judgment of progress and focuses on process as well as product. Teachers can use such techniques as reading/writing logs, journals, tape recordings, running records, and other observational methods to supplement traditional teacher- or publisher-made end of unit tests.

TABLE 1.3 Typical Formative Evaluation Questions

Student Outcomes	How has the addition of a computerized math explorations laboratory affected student attitudes and outcomes in required math courses?
	What changes in student motivation and perceptions of ability are occurring in our ungraded primary classrooms?
	What changes could we make in the homeroom guidance program to improve school attendance?
Curriculum	What required literature books should be retained next year? Dropped? Made optional?
	How can curriculum goals and expectations for student performance better meet student needs?
	What changes do we need to make to provide challenging problem-solving experiences for all students in all subjects?
	What enrichment can be added to the mathematics program to prepare students enrolled in grade-8 math for algebra?
Instruction	How can we provide instruction in the content areas to limited-English-proficient students?
	What strategies have worked best to help low-achieving students keep up in heterogeneously grouped classes?
Staff	What kinds of problems has staff had in implementing portfolio assessment? In translating portfolios to grades?
	Which staff members can be used to provide coaching for others in the use of math manipulatives and meaning-based math activities?
Parents and Community	How can parent volunteers be used more effectively?
	What changes do we need to make in advisory council procedures to get more parent participation?
School Climate	How can we improve school spirit and extracurricular participation?
	What parts of the dropout prevention program are most directly linked to students staying in school?

Select and Refine Priority Questions

You may find you are interested in many more questions than you have the time, energy, or wherewithal to address. During the focusing stage of the evaluation, however, you should allow yourself to be as inclusive as possible. Allow your advisory group to brainstorm a range of questions about each aspect of program quality in which you are interested (student outcomes, curriculum, instruction, climate, and so on).

You may wish to use Worksheet 1.1, "Evaluation Focus and Priority Questions" (see Resource D for the blank version; a filled-in example appears in Sample Worksheet 1.1) to provide a structure for this brainstorming session. Write down one to three (at most) general questions you would like to answer in a program area. Then be as specific as you can about what you mean by each of these questions. For example, simply asking "How are we doing in student outcomes?" is too vague. Even asking "How are students achieving in reading?" is too vague. Try to specify what you mean by student success in reading—standardized test performance, oral reading, motivation, reading for pleasure? Similarly, don't simply pose a question such as "How good is our school climate?" Instead, pose a series of questions that indicate what's important to you in school climate—relations among students, between teachers and students, among teachers, achievement expectations, and the like.

Or, if you are oriented toward formative evaluation, trying to track the effects of programmatic changes or of innovative programs, formulate specific evaluation questions that apply directly to how and what your program is trying to accomplish. For example, you would not simply want to pose the general question: "Is our dropout program accomplishing intended student outcomes?" but would want to ask questions about the specific outcomes the program was intended to influence—for example, are students remaining in school? Is their attendance improving? Are their grades improving? Similarly, while the extent of program implementation is a critical issue, you would not want to leave your question at this level of generality. Instead, you would want to ask about whether critical program features are being implemented as intended—for instance, are counselors meeting regularly with identified students? Are students attending after-school tutorials? Are parents actively involved in their children's program? Have identified community agencies been actively involved in the program?

Although articulating specific questions of interest is an arduous and time-consuming process, it is time well spent. It will immeasurably help you in selecting appropriate progress measures that are sensitive to your school's goals. It also will help you to communicate to others exactly what you are trying to accomplish, helping to focus not only your assessment efforts but your programmatic efforts as well. Furthermore, posing specific questions will encourage you to be realistic about your program expectations and about posing reasonable evaluation questions—questions that are manageable and feasible to answer.

After you have generated your list, put a check next to all mandatory questions: those you must answer to fulfill district or state requirements or to meet the goals set in your school plan. Next, decide the priority rankings for the other questions.

How do you decide which questions are most important or should be given highest priority? No answer fits all situations. Michael

Sample Worksheet 1.1
Evaluation Focus and Priority Questions

	Priority Rating			
Questions	*Low*	*Medium*	*High*	*Required*
Outcomes:				
How does our dropout rate compare with that of the state?				✓
Which students are "at risk" in terms of high school credits, attendance, and GPA?			✓	
What is student attitude toward school completion?		✓		
Curriculum:				
Are "at-risk students" enrolled in our study skills program?	✓			
What materials are being used with at-risk students in heterogeneously grouped English and social studies classes?			✓	
Instruction:				
What special strategies do teachers have for helping at-risk students within regular classrooms?			✓	
To what extent are teachers implementing the "Teacher Expectation-Student Success Program" strategies?		✓		
Staff:				
What does the staff identify as causing our dropout rate?			✓	
Parents and Community:				
In what ways can parents be involved in reducing our dropout rate?				✓

Patton (1988) suggests that the screening criteria for any evaluation question should be these: "What do I want to know that I don't already know?" and "What will it enable me to do that I can't do already?" We have found the most useful questions about outcomes are those that focus on outcomes highly valued by particular stakeholder groups. As for questions related to school climate, curriculum, instruction, staff, and parents/community, select those examining processes that are

- most essential to program success or school effectiveness,
- most complex/difficult to accomplish,

- most costly or resource intensive,
- most controversial, and/or
- related to more than one valued outcome.

Try to limit your "high-priority" designation to three or four questions, at most, in the program area of interest. That way, if you have been overambitious, you can adjust your focus. Remember, too, that you will be revising your questions and making them clearer as you progress in your evaluation. The instruments you choose and the settings in which you use them could cause you to rethink or reword your guiding questions.

Once you have a set of manageable mandatory or high-priority questions, you are ready to consider how you will answer them—our task in Step Two.

References

Berman, P., & McLaughlin, M. W. (1978). *Federal programs supporting educational change: Implementing and sustaining innovations* (Vol. 3). Santa Monica, CA: Rand Corporation.

Bredenkamp, S. (Ed.). (1987). *Developmentally appropriate practice in early childhood programs serving children from birth through age 8.* Washington, DC: National Association for the Education of Young Children.

Hord, S. M., Rutherford, W. L., Huling-Austin, L., & Hall, G. E. (1987). *Taking charge of change.* Alexandria, VA: Association for Supervision and Curriculum Development.

Patton, M. Q. (1988). *Utilization-focused evaluation* (2nd ed.). Newbury Park, CA: Sage

Suggested Readings

Our suggestions in this section include two kinds of resources: Those designed to help you ask useful questions and narrow the scope of your evaluation, and those describing action theories underlying the curriculum. Knowledge of these action theories should precede formative evaluation activities. If you wonder at the relative length of this list, it reflects the relative amount of time needed in focusing activities.

Brandt, Ronald S. (Ed.). (1981). *Applied strategies for curriculum evaluation.* Alexandria, VA: Association for Supervision and Curriculum Development.

Although this book only focuses on one aspect of school-level evaluation—the curriculum—it provides a variety of examples from practitioners that can serve as models for particular school settings.

Bredenkamp, S. (Ed.). (1987). *Developmentally appropriate practice in early childhood programs serving children from birth through age 8.* Washington, DC: National Association for the Education of Young Children.
A staple in the library of early childhood or elementary education, this book provides the theoretical foundations for a developmental, child-centered curriculum. The specific developmentally appropriate practices listed can guide program development and review.

California Curriculum Frameworks. Sacramento, CA: Department of Education.
So you don't live in California and never would. Nevertheless, the state's Department of Eduction has produced a series of curriculum frameworks for each curriculum area from art to zoology. These frameworks incorporate the latest research in student learning, curriculum organization, and assessment. The guidelines define "good" programs for today's students.

Davis, R. B., Maher, C. A., & Noddings, M. (Eds.). (1990). *Constructivist views on the teaching and learning of mathematics.* Reston, VA: National Council of Teachers of Mathematics (NCTM).
For those who simply must know more, this monograph in the *Journal for Research in Mathematics Education* introduces the theory behind "hands-on" or meaning-based mathematics instruction, explores mathematical thinking, and describes how students engage in mathematics. It provides suggestions for teachers as well—the real *theory* behind current mathematics curriculum theory.

Morris, L. L., & Fitz-Gibbon, C. T. (1978). *How to deal with goals and objectives.* Beverly Hills, CA: Sage.
A step-by-step approach to writing and using goals and objectives in the evaluation process. For groups unused to thinking about measurable or observable progress indicators, this book is a boon.

National Council of Teachers of Mathematics. (1989). *Curriculum and evaluation standards for school mathematics.* Reston, VA: NCTM.
An essential document for reviewing mathematics programs, it has served as a model for many state mathematics frameworks and is a resource for the development of national mathematics tests as part of the President's "America 2000" agenda.

National Council of Teachers of Mathematics. (1991). *Professional standards for teaching mathematics.* Reston, VA: NCTM.
This is the companion volume to the NCTM *Curriculum Standards.* It is useful in program development and for looking at your own instructional practices, and it can serve as a guideline for professional development programs.

Routman, R. (1991). *Invitations: Changing as teachers and learners K-12.* Portsmouth, NH: Heinemann Educational.

This is the quintessential practitioner's guide to whole language instruction written by a public school language arts teacher. It presents whole language theory and teaching and evaluation strategies. The "evaluation" chapter is essential, describing what happens to standardized test scores (for those who don't already know) when whole language programs constitute the curriculum. This chapter provides specific alternative assessment and evaluation strategies for K-12 whole language/English/humanities programs.

Stecher, B. M., & Davis, W. A. (1987). *How to focus an evaluation.* Newbury Park, CA: Sage.

Tailor-made for this first step, this volume of the *Program Evaluation Kit* provides administrators working with advisory groups with the background needed to guide the process of selecting evaluation questions.

Stufflebeam, D. L., McCormick, C. H., Brinkerhoff, R. O., & Nelson, C. O. (1985). *Conducting educational needs assessment.* Boston, MA: Kluwer Nijhoff.

From one of the pioneers in educational evaluation comes advice for educators struggling with identifying information needs and important constituencies for school evaluation.

2

Step Two
Identify Tracking Strategies

Overview

In Step One, you selected areas of interest, such as student outcomes and school climate, as a focus for your school improvement efforts. You also identified a couple of specific evaluation questions in each of these areas. The task in this second step is to find appropriate strategies to help you answer these questions. Continue working with your small group of key personnel, your advisory council, department heads, or the like, to address three questions that are central to identifying tracking strategies:

- What evidence are we looking for?
- Where and how are we going to find it?
- What standards will we use to judge our success?

What Evidence Are We Looking For?

A first challenge in identifying appropriate tracking strategies is pinpointing the specific qualities or changes for which you are looking. What are the behavioral manifestations of the qualities in which we're interested? What are the critical things we can observe to know whether desired changes are occurring? What are the specifics of what we want to know? Although these perhaps seem like simple and straightforward issues, you may find they are neither. Like other steps in the evaluation process, you may find instead that the process of addressing these issues raises some interesting discussions about what are truly key and meaningful aspects of your school program. You will need to think hard and creatively about what is essential information for answering each of your evaluation questions.

The starting point, again, is your evaluation questions. Do they suggest the kinds of evidence you will need? For example, if you are looking at your dropout prevention program and have asked whether counselors are effectively meeting with students on a regular basis, you might want to look at the number of appointments counselors have had with your target group since the beginning of school and at whether the meetings are perceived as effective. Getting more precise, you also would want to consider the specific qualities that should count as effective—such as the nature of the interactions between students and counselors and the content of the sessions. Furthermore, if you asked whether attendance was improving for these at-risk students, you will obviously need attendance data. If you want to know whether students' attitudes toward school are improving, you might look at attendance, homework completion, or classroom behavior or whether students say they "like" school.

To take another example, suppose your interests center on a program aimed at cultural sensitivity and integration and that one of your questions inquires about whether race relations are improving. You might look at whom students choose to eat lunch with, whom they socialize with during and after school, whom they choose to work with in class when given the opportunity, or whom they say they would like to study with, join a club with, or some other question related to affiliation.

What you are trying to define are "indicators" that will give you meaningful data to answer *your* questions. Although there certainly is no single correct set of such indicators, Table 2.1 offers a range that may be appropriate for answering some of yours. Note that the table concentrates mainly on indicators of student outcomes; your efforts will want to consider other aspects as well.

Where and How Are We Going to Find Our Evidence?

As Table 2.1 demonstrates, what we want to know is often closely tied to the specifics of how we will collect our information. For example, when we are interested in attendance data, the natural source is student attendance records. If we are concerned with perceptions about different aspects of our program, asking relevant constituencies about their perceptions is a natural option, either through an interview or a questionnaire. As these examples show, in deciding where to get our evidence, we have two major choices: to use existing sources of information or to develop the means to gather new information.

What's already available?

Concerns for time and resources often dictate that we first ask: "What information do we already have that is related to our evaluation questions?" Do we have records (or could we fairly easily devise ways

TABLE 2.1 Sample Progress Tracking Indicators

Descriptive Indicators	*At School*	*At District*
Student ethnicity	✓	
Student language proficiency	✓	
Student education code: gifted, special education		✓
AFDC count		✓
Parent occupation	✓	
School capacity and facility information		✓
Teacher credentialing: majors, minors, status		✓
Specialist/resource staff	✓	
Program Characteristics		
Number enrolled in gifted, special education, bilingual programs	✓	
Course objectives and required texts	✓	✓
Enrollment patterns: requirements, electives	✓	
Grading patterns: grade distributions by class/teacher		✓
Recent program changes: goals/text/strategies	✓	
School Climate / Student Attitudes		
Course evaluations	✓	
Principal observations of teachers being evaluated this year	✓	
Parent comments and phone calls	✓	
Program review report or state accreditation report		✓
Student Outcomes		
Droput rate		✓
Average daily attendance	✓	
Post-high school placement: college, military, work	✓	
Standardized test scores: state, national	✓	
Percentage receiving "D," "F," or "Unsatisfactory"	✓	
Retention rate (including 2-year kindergartners)	✓	
Course-related tests: advanced placement, Regents, teacher tests	✓	
Work-experience placement: kinds of jobs, retention, evaluations	✓	

to obtain them) of attendance, club membership, counseling appointments? Do we have computerized summaries of grade point averages, a "D/F/Unsatisfactory" list of students who are getting poor marks? Where have we filed our reports from the ACT or SAT testing programs? Does our state testing program provide information related to the performance of "at-risk" students, of limited English students, of students new to the school? Do we have records on library check-outs, on college acceptances, on attendance and ratings of teacher in-service days, and so on? As we've all no doubt noticed, the record keeping and bureaucratic requirements in schools these days produce lots of records, some of which may be relevant to our evaluation issues. The bad news is that those records may be deeply buried, unevenly maintained, or constructed in such a way that they yield unwieldy data. So, while you first consider available data to answer your questions, do so with care and with consideration of their accuracy, accessibility, completeness, and utility.

Who can we ask?

Another strategy for gathering evidence is to consider: "Who might provide a credible answer to our questions?" Should we ask parents or teachers to report whether they have noticed any improvements in student attitude toward school? Should we interview some key students about how they feel about school? Do we ask counselors to provide anecdotes related to their meetings with students and about student attitudes toward school? Would community members be a good source of information for some of our questions? Does the district office have any records that might be useful? In other words, who are knowledgeable sources of information?

How can we get the information?

Closely related to the issue of who there is to ask is that of how to get relevant information from them. There are many possible alternatives:

- Should we administer *questionnaires*—to teachers, parents, students, community members, others? Should we use structured or open-ended questions?
- Should we conduct *interviews*? Should this be done individually or in small groups (often called "focus groups")? Will we use structured or open-ended questions?
- What about *attitude measures* or other inventories? Do we try to make our own? Are there some we might adapt from other schools? Are there any that are commercially available that might be appropriate?
- Would *observations* using checklists or open-ended techniques help us answer our questions?
- What about students' *work samples, portfolios, special performances,* and so on?
- Are there *alternative measures* that have been developed by other schools or districts that might suit our needs or could be adapted to them?
- Are there other *creative strategies* for getting the information we need? What about videos or audiotaped interviews?

Select Tracking Strategies by Balancing Competing Requirements

Credibility. In deciding which strategies are best, again, there is no single right answer. Issues of data quality and of credibility of information are certainly paramount, but, unfortunately, what is credible to one important constituency may not be so to another. For example, the general public and many parents put a lot of faith in standardized test scores whereas teachers who work with tests on a regular basis know the limitations of such test information. On the other hand, teacher observations of student work over a period of time can provide rich and credible information about student progress and status to other teachers and to school administrators but are difficult to summarize for outside audiences and sometimes viewed as suspect by them. Although, ideally, you want to be responsive to the needs of all of your important constituencies, the reality of available time, expertise, and measures will impose important limitations on your instrument selections.

Validity. In addition to which measures can provide information that is both credible and feasible to collect, your selection of instruments must consider very carefully the concept of "validity." Validity is largely a question of whether a measure actually measures what it is intended to measure and whether its results can provide accurate inferences for the decision(s) at hand. In the case of our evaluation planning, a key validity concern is the match between the information provided by the instrument and what we want to know—the inferences we want to draw from the results. For example, if we are using results of a published, standardized mathematics test to assess our school's effectiveness in teaching mathematics, one important validity issue is whether the content of the test reflects essential knowledge and understanding in mathematics; another is the match between the test content and our school curriculum. Without this match, the test provides information that essentially is irrelevant to our concerns. Similarly, in trying to track the process of implementing a new program at our school, validity demands that there be a good match between the intended key processes of your program and the specific items used to assess them.

The sensitivity of your instruments to what you are trying to accomplish, in short, is critical to your assessment. It also is critical to your ability to demonstrate your success and to uncover true strengths and weaknesses.

Feasibility and ease of data collection therefore need to be carefully balanced by concerns for validity. For example, using readily available standardized test score data and attendance data gleaned from last year's rosters could save a significant amount of time that would otherwise have to be devoted to instrument development or data collection. The price, however, could be insensitivity to school goals and intentions for the first measure and inaccuracy for the other.

Recent changes in curriculum increase the possibility of mismatches between curriculum and existing tests. Often, the two are grounded in different philosophies of learning and different psychological theories. Some whole language advocates, for example, take issue with the design of standardized tests built on the theory that reading is the acquisition of a sequence of discrete skills. They believe that these tests cannot measure valued literacy skills. Many mathematics educators have expressed similar concerns about the content of many existing standardized mathematics tests.

Innovative measures.

When the test and the program are not congruent, other indicators of progress are a necessity. Student writing performance, the number of books read, work samples, or entire portfolios of work, parent or teacher observations, or parent satisfaction with student progress are some of the many possibilities that could be substituted for or added to standardized test scores.

Growing concerns with existing standardized tests, in fact, have given rise to an explosion of interest in developing new, performance-based measures of student outcomes. As mentioned, these include student work samples, science demonstrations, extended projects, speeches, collections of essays and other work samples affectionately known as *portfolios,* and the like. Data from these sources have the advantage of providing actual samples of meaningful student work that can provide insights into student thinking processes. But work samples and work collections take time to judge. Criteria need to be developed and agreed upon, and scorers must be trained to apply scoring guidelines consistently across papers. Despite the time and effort, however, teachers often say that the time spent in defining program goals, in specifying performance expectations, in generating scoring criteria, and in actually scoring the samples is great staff development because it helps them to agree on what their programs are trying to do, and they can apply the methods to their own classrooms. A second by-product of collecting work samples is the identification of model student work that will become exemplars for teaching next year's students.

Look for growing resources in the area of alternative measures of student performance. Many states, districts, and even schools, as well as research and development agencies and test publishers, currently are involved in systematic development efforts. These will yield measures that can be adopted in full or adapted to local school needs.

Self report instruments. Questionnaires and interviews are standard, tried-and-true methods for directly asking about issues of interest. Questionnaires can be a relatively fast and cost-effective way to find out directly what you want to know, albeit sometimes at a somewhat superficial level. Often, you can adapt a questionnaire used by another school for your own purposes at little cost. (Resources A and B at the end of the book include sample teacher and parent questionnaires from a middle school that you could adapt to suit your information needs.) Although it does take time to design clear questions and summarize results, as well as patient follow-up to assure adequate return rates, the result can be information that is tailored to your specific evaluation questions.

Interviews, by phone or in person, have the common-sense design appeal of questionnaires and, at higher cost, can yield deeper understanding of issues of interest. With trained and persistent interviewers, you can assure adequate return rates and can bypass potential problems in respondents' reading ability.

Observations. Formal observations are a little more intimidating to design because they require you to get very specific about the types of actions or types of behavior you are interested in or expect to see as a result of your program. They also require careful analysis of when, where, and how often you expect to see such actions; consideration of reasonable times for observation; and repeated observations to assure reliability of measurement. Conducted by trained and impartial observers, however, systematic observations can yield highly credible data on what's actually happening in your school and its programs—rather than what people say is happening (the latter is colored by social desirability and by respondents' notions of what they think should be happening).

Similar to interviews, observations require significant amounts of observer time and thorough training. Combined with the need for careful development and repeated observations to assure reliable results, formal observations are a costly data collection strategy. Whether or not formal observations are part of our data collection strategy, our informal observations, gathered continuously over the program and focused specifically on programmatic areas of interest, are invaluable for making sense of results and refining program effectiveness.

Feasibility and credibility trade-offs. Unfortunately, concerns for feasibility and credibility often push us in opposing directions. Feasible often means inexpensive, "quick and dirty," something that can be accomplished by local staff on top of existing responsibilities—such as teacher-made or school-developed surveys that have not been subjected to technical scrutiny. If you are worried about the credibility of your results, you may have to bring in an independent evaluator to help with instrument development and validation processes.

Use Multiple Information Sources to Address Each Question

There is so such thing as a perfect instrument, and even the best ones reflect error as well as truth. Because of inherent errors in any instrument, it is highly advisable to use more than one source to gather information related to each of your evaluation questions. The advantage lies both in the validity of your findings and in their credibility to various audiences. As summarized in Table 2.2, each information source has its weaknesses and is vulnerable to criticism by those not agreeing with its findings. If several sources provide similar results, confidence in your findings will be strengthened.

What Standards Will We Use?

At the same time you select ways to gather information related to your questions, you should be asking yourself and/or your advisory group, "What standards will indicate that we are making progress?" Although it may seem premature to be worrying now about standards for making judgments, it is not. Your standards will have important implications for what information you will collect and from whom, and therefore they are essential to devising an appropriate data collection strategy.

Evaluators typically use one or more of the following strategies to find out whether programs are improving or need revision.

Look for change over time.

Here, the primary issue often is whether things are improving; if they are, we can consider ourselves successful. Furthermore, when we observe a trend over time, we can be more confident that something is indeed occurring in our program than if we just take a one-time-only snapshot. Are student test scores, after adjusting for changes in student population or test norms, getting better? Are scores better than before we implemented our improvement plan? Are parents more satisfied with and involved in our school? Are new instructional techniques being used two years after the in-service?

If change over time is important, we need to know where we stood prior to the start of a new program and then use the same or parallel measures at regular intervals to measure our progress.

Look for improvement relative to some comparison group.

Here, the issue is how our program and its outcomes compare with those of others who are similar to us—or others who represent goals to which we aspire. Success can be defined in terms of a favorable comparison. Are our students achieving at the same or better levels than students in similar schools? How do we compare with state or national norms? How do we compare with "distinguished" schools or other model programs? If a comparison is implied by our evaluation question, we must select an appropriate comparison group.

TABLE 2.2 Selecting Evaluation Instruments

	Advantages	*Limitations*
Questionnaires	Can probe several aspects of the program on one measure Can get candid, anonymous comments and suggestions if space provided for comments Questions are standardized for all respondents Questions can be made selected response for quick, machine scoring Gives respondents time to think	Not as flexible as interviews People often express themselves better orally than in writing Responding is often tedious and people forget to return questionnaires People may give "socially desirable" responses Requires literacy Depth of information sometimes sacrificed for breadth
Interviews	Can do by phone at times convenient to respondents Allows people who can't read or write to answer Can be conducted in respondents' native language Flexible; can pursue unanticipated lines of query Depth; can probe responses Persistence can yield high return rates	Time-consuming, thus costly Possible for interviewer to (consciously or unconsciously) influence responses People may give "socially desirable" responses
Observations	Can use required observations (such as teacher evaluation) for other purposes Observers can see what teachers or others actually do, not what they say they do	Time needed to develop observation measure and train observers Presence of observers may influence classroom behavior Time needed to conduct a sufficient number of observations Scheduling problems Costly

continued

TABLE 2.2 Continued

	Advantages	*Limitations*
Performance Tests Essays Demonstrations Projects Performances (music, dance, drama, speech)	Provide actual sample of student work Can provide "diagnostic" information about student performance and about instruction Available for all subjects (unlike standardized tests) Credible method for assessing complex skills and processes Contextualized and relevant to real-life situations	Criteria for judging needs to reflect subject matter standards yet be understandable and usable by all Need many samples to draw conclusions about one individual; classroom/school inferences require fewer samples Scoring process is time-consuming Finding scorers may be difficult given the time commitment to training and scoring Costly if you pay scorers or use release time
Portfolios	Provide a broader range of student work than one sample Can be used for many purposes Provide students opportunities to observe own growth and reflect on own work Encourage integration of instruction and assessment	What constitutes a portfolio must be defined Scoring methods must be developed Costly to score Methods for interpreting need to be developed
Archival Information Test scores from prior years Attendance Discipline records Teacher records	Records already exist No administration or development costs	Gathering information takes clerical time May be incomplete, inconsistent May not have exactly the information you need
Published Achievement and Attitude Measures	No development cost Information available about validity and reliability Most are quickly scored Clear methods for interpreting results Inexpensive to score	May not match local goals Item formats often don't match real-life tasks Provide little diagnostic information

Against whom should we judge ourselves? Table 2.3 summarizes some possible comparisons that help answer typical evaluation questions.

Try to achieve an absolute level of performance on goals.

Sometimes we have a very good idea of what specific goals we are trying to accomplish, such as all students taking and passing certain courses or all students being able to communicate effectively in writing. Perhaps our goals are to have at least five teachers using whole language techniques in the primary grades or to have at least half of our students enrolled in Algebra 1 by grade 10.

To assess whether we are meeting absolute standards, we need to consider what are reasonable yet "high" or positive expectations. Standards need to be high enough to be meaningful but not unattainable.

In reality, we most often use several approaches to standards in judging and reporting the success of our school. For example, we might have an absolute standard that we hope to achieve over time and will not be fully satisfied until we achieve it (e.g., all students successfully completing high school). Nonetheless, we will count ourselves successful if we make continuous and significant progress toward that standard.

Worksheet 2.1 provides a format for recording the results of the session(s) in which you decide, by whatever means, what information you want to answer your evaluation questions, from whom and how you might get it, and your standards for success. With these tracking strategies firmly in hand, you are ready to schedule your data collection process, the central task in Step Three. (An example of tracking strategies for a whole-language program appears in Sample Worksheet 2.1.)

Suggested Readings

Given our training and occupations, we had to exercise severe restraint in our recommendations for this section. With norm-referenced standardized tests under attack, alternative assessment guides are being produced exponentially. We urge you to attend meetings of your professional organization to keep on top of the quickly changing scene.

Fowler, F. J. (1984). *Survey research methods.* Beverly Hills, CA: Sage.

None of us escapes survey development. If you want to know how to do it "right," use this guide. All bases are covered from sampling, to question development, to data analysis and ethical issues.

Henerson, M. E., Morris, L. L., & Fitz-Gibbon, C. T. (1987). *How to measure attitudes.* Newbury Park, CA: Sage.

Another essential from the Sage *Program Evaluation Kit*, this book deals with how to find or develop attitude measures as well as limitations in interpreting attitude data.

Sample Worksheet 2.1 Tracking Strategies			
Evaluation Questions	1. How far along are we in implementing integrated instruction for social studies, language arts, math, and the arts? 2. What support do teachers need to integrate instruction? 3. Is student performance in reading, math, and writing improving in integrated instruction settings? 4. Are special populations, special education, LEP, and gifted students being served appropriately? 5. What has been the impact of our parent involvement program? 6. What do we need to do to improve the program next year?		
Questions	*Evidence of Progress*	*Source of Information (Instruments)*	*Standards of Success*
1, 2, 6	Teachers using cooperative learning groups, student choices within activities, multiple groups, teachers coaching, subjects indistinguishable	Informal observations	All teachers using cooperative learning; at least one "choice" activity per unit
3, 4	Fail rates for special education and LEP students	Competency test	Fail rate in writing drops
3, 4	Average percentile ranks in math, reading, written expression	State assessment, Nationally standardized test	Higher than last year
5	Number of parent volunteers	Teachers' volunteer logs	At least 10 hours a month
5	Attendance at parent education meetings	Sign-in sheets for November, February, and June meetings	At least 60 parents per meeting
5	Parent satisfaction rating of program	Parent survey	Satisfaction rating (average of survey questions 3, 4, 7) of 80% or higher

Lindheim, E., Morris, L. L., & Fitz-Gibbon, C. T. (1987). *How to measure performance and use tests.* Newbury Park, CA: Sage
A companion to the measuring attitudes book, this book serves as a valuable resource for selecting or developing measures. This

TABLE 2.3 Methods for Determining Standards of Success

Evaluation Question	*Ways of Looking at Information to Determine Standards of Success*
Needs Assessment How are students doing? What are our strengths? What areas need improvement?	Average student performance compared with average performance of students in schools like ours
	Proportion of students scoring in different quartile ranges or receiving each score on a performance test scoring rubric compared with the distribution of scores at similar schools
	Average scores compared with our performance in the past
	The distribution of scores/positive questionnaire ratings compared with the past (3-5 years)
	Average performance (mean or median score) compared with the state or national average on the same measure(s)
	Average performance (mean or median) compared with a standard/goal set by the state, nation, or other agency (e.g., a "3" on advanced placement exams is "passing")
	Distributions of scores/proportions compared with state, national, or other standards (e.g., national goal that all adults will be literate)
Formative Evaluation Is the program being implemented as planned? How can we improve the program?	Percentage of content match of courses with required state frameworks or national curriculum association guidelines (e.g., NCTM *Curriculum and Evaluation Standards*)
	Match of curriculum as implemented to intended implementation plan as described by a funding proposal, monitoring agency, or school program description
	Comparison of classroom observations with what staff says they are doing
	Comparison of program activities/ outcomes with community expectations as described in parent meetings, kinds of parent concerns about the program (e.g., complaints about not enough homework)
	Comparison of program with similar programs that have been identified as "exemplars"

volume of the *Program Evaluation Kit* provides sources for tracking down published tests as well as steps in developing performance tests. Of interest is the section listing sources for published tests in a wide range of fields from vocational education, to foreign language, home economics, and physical education.

Popham, W. J. (1981). *Modern educational measurement.* Englewood Cliffs, NJ: Prentice-Hall.
Written in the same lively, engaging style as his evaluation book, Popham's measurement text provides the conceptual foundation and an overview of test development procedures for the major kinds of assessment devices: criterion-referenced tests, norm-referenced tests, attitude surveys, and essays. Although not a step-by-step manual, the book explains central concepts in measurement clearly and helps evaluators understand the strengths and limitations of their tools.

Tierney, R. J., Carter, M. A., & Desai, L. E. (1991). *Portfolio assessment in the reading-writing classroom.* Norwood, MA: Christopher-Gordon.
This is one of the first of the surely many to come dealing with portfolio assessment. Although the examples are from English language arts, they apply throughout the curriculum. Of particular interest to the evaluator are chapters on student self-assessment and portfolio analysis and record keeping.

3

Step Three
Manage Instrument Development and Data Collection

Overview

In Step Three, you will select or develop instruments for gathering the data you need to answer your evaluation questions and then proceed to collect information from your population or sample of interest. The central tasks in this step are planning, scheduling, and monitoring. Thorough planning is a necessity as Murphy, of Murphy's Law fame, most certainly is the patron saint of research and evaluation!

With your tracking strategies in hand from Worksheet 2.1, you are ready to select or create the measures you need and then use them to collect your evaluation information. The most efficient strategy for managing the numerous tasks involved with instrument acquisition and data collection is to create a management plan indicating the tasks that need to be accomplished, by whom, and when. Quality data collection requires monitoring. How you record your management plan, whether it is penciled in on your school calendar or whether it is a stand-alone document, is not as important as thinking ahead about how you will accomplish the tasks of selecting or developing instruments and of collecting information to answer your evaluation questions. This step is labor intensive, is time-consuming, and needs to be supervised by someone with an eye for details and a strong streak of perfectionism.

Consolidate Your Evaluation Interests

In Step Two, you were encouraged to brainstorm ways to gather information and advised to use at least two different methods, whenever possible, to strengthen the credibility of your results. The worksheet you used resulted in an evaluation plan that links specific tracking strategies to each of your evaluation questions. As you get down to the nuts and bolts of data collection, you will need to reorganize your plan and shift your focus from the question: "What instruments do I need to address each of my evaluation questions?" to "How should the information I need be distributed by instrument?" Now is the time to review your planned tracking strategies and consolidate them into a feasible number of specific data collection instruments. Look across the information sources you have designated for all of your evaluation questions and find those that frequently recur. You may find, for example, that, while you have several pages of information sources when listed for each question separately, they really boil down to a teacher questionnaire and a parent questionnaire—each addressing a variety of specific issues—and an analysis of various student records. If you have followed our advice on triangulating information sources, you probably also will have identified some issues that are common to several instruments (e.g., planning to ask both parents and teachers about their satisfaction with students' progress in reading, math, liking of school, self-concept, and so on).

Sometimes you will find that you have designated a tracking strategy that is only relevant to one evaluation question or to one or two specific concerns within a single area. If this is the case, then you may want to reassess whether this unique data collection strategy is really necessary or whether needed information could be collected nearly as well through another strategy you're planning to use or through a more cost-effective strategy. For example, suppose you have planned to do a parent survey to address numerous evaluation questions and have designated a community survey to answer a single question about available opportunities for community service and about satisfaction with student preparation. If these are critically important issues to your evaluation or if you feel that surveying the community will send an important message to them, then, by all means, stick to your plans. If, however, these are relatively peripheral issues, then you may want to address these issues through your parent survey and a few well-placed calls to community service agencies. (You might also wrack your brain about whether such information may be available through other means—for example, community agencies may already have gathered data on service opportunities.)

Create a Blueprint for Instrument Development or Instrument Selection

Worksheet 3.1 asks you to designate, across all your evaluation questions, all the issues that need to be addressed by each data collection strategy. For example, in reviewing Worksheet 2.1, you might find that you designated a parent questionnaire for gathering information relevant to questions 1, 2, and 3 and listed specific indications for each; here, in Worksheet 3.1, you'll want to transfer into one place all the indicators that are planned for the parent questionnaire. In reorganizing your evaluation questions by the data collection instruments needed to answer them, you will have created a basic blueprint for each instrument. This instrument blueprint will be an invaluable tool for selecting or developing appropriate instruments.

Remember that the match between your instruments and the issues you plan to address is a critical requirement for validity. If your plan is to select from among available measures, the blueprint will help you to find the best fit. If, on the other hand, you plan to develop your own customized instruments, the blueprint will help you stay focused and write or adapt items that meet your primary and specific interests. Whether you select or develop instruments, you will need to pay attention to a range of factors that influence data quality, such as reliability, test administration considerations, appropriateness for your population, and content quality.

Create a Consolidated Management Plan

A consolidated list of needed instruments is also a good starting place for your management plan. By designating when you plan to use each instrument, the steps you will need to complete to be prepared for such use, and who is to be responsible for each step, you help to assure a smooth (or at least as smooth as possible) development and data collection process. Your schedule will be backward chained from when mandated reports are due or from when it makes sense to collect particular kinds of information. If you're trying to assess end of the year progress, it doesn't make sense to collect the information in February!

The steps in your plan will vary somewhat depending on whether you plan to use existing data, to collect information using available instruments, or to create your own instruments. Bear in mind the following:

- If you need to create your own measures, you will need a time line for development, review, pilot testing, and revision. (See Table 3.1 for a sample process.) Be sure to leave adequate time for repeated proofing and for quantity printing.

Sample Worksheet 3.1
Instrument Blueprints

Instrument	*Questions Asked*
Portfolios	What kinds of mathematics problem representations did the students use? What percentage of the assignments represented critical thinking/problem solving? What difficulties with math did students identify in their self-evaluations? What kinds of work did students include for their self-selected samples? What were the range of strategies students used to solve problems?
Parent Questionnaire	Do parents notice a difference in their child's attitude toward mathematics? What kinds of help do parents provide? What kinds of additional help do parents say students need? Do parents understand the purpose of the new mathematics program?
Student Questionnaire	Do students like math? Do students feel competent in math? Where do students say they would like more help? Are top students being challenged?
Faculty Interviews	What difficulties are faculty having setting up "hands-on" lessons? In what ways are faculty integrating mathematics instruction with other subjects? What additional support would faculty like? How do faculty rate the mathematics resources (pattern blocks, beans, rice, and so on)? Do faculty notice any differences in student attitudes? Ability to keep up?
Standardized Nationally Normed	What are student average standard scores in math problem solving? Concepts? What are student average standard scores in these areas for special education, gifted, and LEP students? What items pose the most difficulty? What kinds of mistakes do students tend to make on selected response tests and why?
State Assessment	What kinds of answers did our students give on the open-ended math question? What is our average score in math problem solving? How did kids do in geometry concepts? In number concepts?
Competency	What strategies did students use when answering the competency essay about solving the open-ended problem? What was the average percentage getting the five problems correct?
Other	What kinds of questions appear on teacher-made, end of unit tests? What kinds of teacher-developed questions gave students the most difficulty? How does progress on classroom tests compare with portfolio ratings and standardized tests?

- Where you are using commercial instruments or those developed by others, be sure to leave yourself adequate time for ordering, shipping, and distributing materials.
- If you are collecting existing information (e.g., information from student cumulative records), you will need to create user-friendly and summary-friendly forms for recording the data.
- If data collection requires special skills or orientation, be sure to leave adequate time to develop training for and deliver it to data collectors.

Lest the instrument development or selection process sound too complicated, remember that much of your information probably will come from already existing measures, such as mandated tests, teacher-assigned student work samples, or projects; from routinely collected data such as attendance, textbook expenditure, or counseling referrals; or from adapted surveys that spring rather easily from your specific evaluation questions. For most of us, "instrument development" means finding a parent questionnaire or interview used by another school or district and adapting it for our own purposes. The time line for adaptation, also provided in Table 3.1, is considerably shorter than that for development "from scratch." And, for those of you wishing to get a head start, we have included sample parent, teacher, and student questionnaires in Resources A, B, and C. Adapt these if they fit your situation and, as you encounter examples from other schools, add them to these questionnaires for later reference.

Having determined the general tasks that need to be completed, you need to decide who will have primary responsibility for each as well as the important milestones for scheduling. This task-person time line becomes your data collection management plan. But, before you formalize this plan, you will need to consider who will be involved in administering measures (and whether they will need to be hired and/or trained); whether you will administer your instruments to a sample or to the entire population; whether your plan requires a comparison group for whom data must be collected; and when the optimal time to collect the data is.

Sample Worksheet 3.2 presents a sample management plan. It contains the key information that the evaluation coordinator needs at a glance: Who is getting what from whom and when? The plan also helps you to identify potential bottlenecks in the data collection process. October, November, and April appear to be busy months. Should you reschedule some of your April evaluation activities—especially in light of some of the other activities that you know will be occurring at your school? Should you begin instrument development a little earlier or later? Should you consider purchasing or adapting extant measures to hasten the development process (and lighten the burden)? Your data collection plan will not answer these questions,

text continued on page 54

TABLE 3.1 Data Collection Time Lines for Commonly Used Evaluation Instruments

	Type of Instrument			
Time	*Already Published Tests*	*Archival Information (attendance; past scores; CUM information)*	*School Developed: Selected Response*	*School-Developed Performance (includes observations, projects, essays, portfolios)*
6 months prior	Take inventory Order needed materials	Locate records; determine what's missing and how to "fill in" if possible	If starting from scratch, develop questions and response alternatives; try out with sample, revise	Preferably a **year** prior, convene a committee to discuss tasks and scoring criteria; pilot tasks, scoring, and rater training
3 months prior	Preslug answer sheets with student ID, grade, other needed info	Monitor filing of current data	Adapt already existing survey; try out survey items with sample; revise; translate and try with bilingual sample	Develop administration procedures; develop descriptions for students to understand task (sample items and scoring criteria)
1 month prior	Discuss uniform test preparation guidelines with teachers; explain content, consequences; and discuss ethical preparation guidelines	Meet with advisory group to determine exactly what information is needed (grade, sex, teacher, month, and so on); assign codes for these items	Write cover letter for mailed surveys; write administration directions for tests, school surveys	Produce materials; count and distribute; meet with teachers to explain administration procedures
2 weeks prior	Prepare test administration directions	Practice summarizing data to iron out bugs in coding procedures	Run mailing labels; print surveys/tests; prepare class sets for teachers	
1 week prior	Distribute testing materials to teachers; go over administration procedures; explain importance of accurate information	Hand out data entry coding sheets to volunteers or other data collectors and explain procedures	Mail surveys; meet with teachers administering tests/surveys	
Data Received	Organize answer sheets for scoring; check accuracy of special codes for processing reports	Make photocopy of data for "backup" and get data entered into computer or summarized	Follow up and track down missing data	Check to see that answer sheets, portfolios, observation forms have codes for grade, name, and so on

Sample Worksheet 3.2
Data Collection Management Plan

Task by Instrument	*Person Responsible*	*Sampling*	*Sept.*	*Oct.*	*Nov.*	*Dec.*	*Jan.*	*Feb.*	*Mar.*	*Apr.*	*May*
Instrument: Math Portfolios Select group to develop/choose Develop tasks and criteria Produce Distribute Administer Score Analyze and interpret	Principal, mentor teacher, district evaluation office	Random—10% grades 3, 4, 5									
Instrument: Math Chapter Tests Select group to develop/choose Develop tasks and criteria Produce Distribute Administer Score Analyze and interpret	Head teacher: grades 3, 4, 5	Copies of all tests; all grades									
Instrument: State Assessment Select group to develop/choose Develop tasks and criteri Produce Distribute Administer Score Analyze and interpret	District testing office	All grade 4									
Instrument: ITBS Select group to develop/choose Develop tasks and criteria Produce Distribute Administer Score Analyze and interpret	District testing office	All grades K-5									

but it will keep them from sneaking up on you and sabotaging your entire operation. Our sample data collection plan was developed after consideration of the following issues:

Delegate responsibility for data collection.

Very often, it is a simple matter to decide who should be involved in collecting information. When you want responses or work samples from students, teachers are the natural data collectors—unless there's some reason to believe that their presence will distort student responses. For example, it is not a good idea to have teachers administer an attitude measure to students that focuses on students' attitude toward their teachers! Data collected from teachers most probably will be coordinated by an administrator, department head, or union representative, depending on the usual procedures in your district or school. The student council could be responsible for distributing and collecting nonconfidential student questionnaires. PTA volunteers, paraprofessionals, or other adults affiliated with the school may be asked to conduct telephone interviews with parents. Classroom observations fall into the administrator's domain, but mentor teachers, union-approved representatives, district office staff, or local graduate students may be recruited if these are acceptable procedures in your particular setting.

When selecting data collection coordinators, you need to select people who understand the need for objective, representative data, who can be expected to be impartial, and who will not try to influence respondents (including students) in any particular way. Your assistants should be nonthreatening to respondents. The truant officer is probably not a good choice for interviewing students with attendance problems. It also helps when data collectors are also well organized and able to handle the distribution and collection of materials without supervision and willing to follow up repeatedly to get the information or responses that are needed. Those who are doing parent telephone interviews, for example, should be prepared to call a number of times to find someone at home and with time to respond.

Decide whether to sample.

Your management plan for data collection identified what information you will collect by whom. At this point, you need to decide whether you will collect information from or about everyone or whether you will sample—that is, randomly select a proportion of the population of interest to be the subjects of your data collection. Should you mail a questionnaire to all parents or only a sample of them? Should you observe all teachers once a month or a sample of teachers on a more frequent basis? Should you collect work samples or tests from all students? Do you want to distribute the testing burden so that all students take some assessments but no student has to take them all? Do you want to distribute the respondent burden so that half the parents get called for interviews but each is administered only one of two interview forms enabling you to find out about a broader range of issues without overly taxing the patience or time of individual respondents? As a general rule, having more respondents or more data points at the school level provides a better technical base for inferences, but concerns about technical quality must be balanced by ever-present concerns about limited resources—the resources of teacher and student time as well as direct dollar expenditures for instrument purchase/duplication, scoring, and other costs.

Although there are ways to technically compute the proportion of total respondents you should have for valid inferences, common sense about what is credible and reasonable goes a long way when making such decisions. If the potential number of respondents for a questionnaire or survey is fewer than 20, it makes little sense to sample. At the other extreme, if there are 500 families at your school, interviewing them all is probably out of the question (although sending a survey home to them all probably isn't). What is a reasonable sample? Balance feasibility and credibility. Ask yourself, "Would I believe the results if they were based on only [half, a third, a quarter] of the school population?"

Also, be sure to think about the number of respondents you will be dealing with as you design any new instruments. For example, if you expect to get responses back from 250 parents, you will want to be sure that their responses are easy to score and summarize. For sample sizes this large, you probably will want to have a majority of your questions in selected response format, where respondents indicate a response on some given scale—agree to disagree, very effective to very ineffective, very satisfied to very unsatisfied—or choose from among given response alternatives. You also will want to investigate the cost of selected response questionnaires that can be used with a Scan-tron or optical scanner. You may purchase "general purpose" questionnaire forms for both machines that will allow your equipment to summarize questionnaire data (as distinct from test data). Even if you have large samples and are relying primarily on selected response items, be sure to include a few open-ended questions to give you a better sense of what people are feeling and why.

Schedule data collection.

Consult your school and district master calendar as you schedule data collection. Scheduling considerations include the following:

- When are accountability reports due?
- When will the information we need be available?
- How much time do we need to design, try out, and administer measures?
- How much time will it take to summarize, analyze, and report the data?

For example, suppose you have to report to your school board at the end of the fiscal year in June about how you spent your school's "innovative program" allocation as well as about the program's results. You plan to use teacher and student questionnaires that your faculty and parent advisory committee will create. You plan to give yourself at least a month to summarize and discuss the meaning of your results, and you need at least three weeks to send out and collect surveys and to follow up on late or missing respondents. You also want to collect the information as late as possible in the school year to give your new program the maximum time "to take," but you don't want to run into the Open House-May testing crunch. You decide, therefore, that late April is a good time for your surveys. Working backward from your tentative administration date, you designate time for the development of draft questionnaires and time for review, revision, duplication, and development of directions for administration. You now find you must begin your first task in October. If you're planning to do complex interviews or to conduct formal observations, you also will need to build in time to develop or find the instrument, to recruit and to train your data collectors, and to give them opportunities to practice using the instrument.

If you're relying on information summarized by others, of course, you're dependent on their schedules, which too often don't match yours. In these cases, you just have to do the best you can, which sometimes means delaying a desired report, submitting a draft that is missing a section, or using available data from prior years.

Cost: An ever-present mediator.

As you do your scheduling and planning, you want to keep in mind the costs of enacting them. Direct costs are fairly easy to estimate. Publishers can provide you with per student costs for test administration and various scoring options. Printers can give you per page copying costs for bulk printing. Costs of mailing out and providing return envelopes for parent surveys can be estimated based on current postal rates. Costs of travel/mileage getting to and from needed data collection sites can be estimated based on prevailing district or school policy. If you have to hire special staff to complete your plans, estimate how much time you will need from them and what their hourly or daily rates are. Special consultants easily can be asked for budgets detailing the costs of their involvement. Scoring and analysis may require the purchase of new software, as may the production of appealing reports. Every item in your time line probably brings with it direct costs. Be sure to be generous in your estimates—everything always seems to take much, much more time and money than we ever expect.

But direct costs are only a part of the picture. Opportunity costs represent another important area of consideration. Using existing staff or even volunteers to work on the evaluation means they are using their time on this and not doing something else. Do they have sufficient available time to do all that is required? Student time also is a major concern, as student time spent in data collection often is time diverted from instruction. This concern may be diminished immeasurably in the case of "alternative assessment" or "performance assessment," where the assessment tasks themselves are thought to be meaningful learning opportunities, often indistinguishable from instruction.

The point is, once you have your plan in hand, you need to consider the costs implied by the plan. Are they reasonable? Are they feasible? If not, you may find you need to rescope your planned effort: delay some issues until next year, switch to some lower-cost data collection strategies, collaborate with other schools or districts to reduce instrument development costs, or entice your local university to give students course credit for helping with your effort. Be creative to cut costs and maximize efficiency! Table 3.2 provides some sample costs of common evaluation needs.

Avoiding Data Collection Disasters

Data collection brings with it many challenges, and, as mentioned in the introduction to this step, it often seems that Murphy's Law is the operant rule: Whatever can go wrong, will! Advance planning and attention to frequent pitfalls, however, can greatly diminish your problems.

Review measures for clarity, relevance, and bias.

Consistent measurement depends upon well-written, unambiguous questionnaire, interview, or test items. Try to anticipate your respondents and the many ways they could misunderstand a test item or question. Be particularly vigilant about attitude survey items that have different meanings in different cultures. For example, we administered a well-known school attitude measure that awarded points for "high self-esteem" for items in which students felt they should speak out in class and make their opinions known or in which students felt they did well or were outstanding in some way. A Chinese graduate student reviewing the instrument mentioned that the well-adjusted Chinese student would lose points on these self-esteem items because "putting yourself forward" was not considered appropriate in China.

Although you could literally second-guess every item on every measure you use, do try to get others with different educational levels, cultural perspectives, or reading ability to review your instruments so that you are presenting all your respondents with an identical task, a task they will interpret similarly and that will carry the same meaning. People within a school tend to use the same jargon, such as *restructuring, literacy, developmentally appropriate,* or *at risk.* These words, however, carry different meanings for some audiences and no meaning at all for others. It is much better to discover a "bad question" before data collection than to lose information you think is important. One of us is involved with an innovative curriculum development-teacher training project and very interested in whether the project has affected the ways in which teachers judge students. On the teacher questionnaire, we asked, "I would use the following observable

TABLE 3.2 Typical Costs Associated With Evaluation

Service or Product	*Cost*
Evaluation consultant	County office: free District office: free University: $250/day Independent: $35-$150/hr.
Data collector: phone calls, observations, coding archival data	$10-$12.50/hr. for a university student
Published test materials	Booklet of items: $3-$5 each Answer sheets: $0.12-$0.15 each
Published test scoring	Scoring service: $.92 for list of scores Additional reports: vary from $0.10 to $1.75 per student
Outside scoring for local selected response test	Set up charge: $200 Scoring and simple reports: $1.75/student
Scoring for performance tests using teachers	Training: minimum 3 hours per essay type depending upon complexity of rubric. Rating: 1 minute per paper for holistic rubric and short essays; 2-3 for longer; up to 5 minutes per paper for multi-scaled rubrics. Calculate time needed by multiplying number of paper/tasks by time per task, then hours for training to get total time needed. Convert to hours. Divide by number of teachers rating to get person-hours. Multiply by teacher hourly rate or cost of substitute per hour to get total cost. (Faint!)
Data analysis expert	Same as rates for evaluation consultant; if data are on a computer disk, cost will be significantly reduced

indicators to measure what my students have learned . . ." and found that literally all teachers—project and nonproject—checked every single one of the indicators listed. We really wanted to know whether project teachers *value* a wider variety of indicators for evaluating (i.e., grading) students. We should have asked: "I use the following observable indicators for grades," followed up with a question as to how each was weighted. Until we saw the teacher responses, it did not occur to us that we were asking the wrong question. Had we tested the item with a few teachers, we would not have lost data by using this loosely worded question.

Building in a review process for your measures not only minimizes different interpretations of the same question, it also helps you find potentially biased or offensive questions. Biased questions are difficult to identify a priori (after all, who of us intends to be biased?) and often don't show up until *after* respondents have returned their answers. A biased item is one to which students with identical ability levels and similar exposure to instruction respond differently. These items generally are few in number. Offensive questions, on the other hand, can be spotted beforehand by knowledgeable reviewers. Items or questions that present racial or sexual stereotypes or that delve into potentially embarrassing issues should be revised. For example, in your review of the dropout program, you want to know what kind of support parents can provide for their child's education. You ask them how many years of education they have had. If your parent community consists of recently arrived, economically disadvantaged immigrants, you will be asking a question that parents may find embarrassing to answer.

Prepare clear directions.

You will also need to have clear directions to respondents and for people administering student measures or conducting observations to standardize administration conditions. You want all people responding to the same measure or being observed to understand the task in the same way so that differences in responses will reflect real differences among people and not simply different interpretations of the same task. Words such as "indicate" are not as clear as instructions to "circle the response" or "write your answer in two sentences." Remember that, while you may understand quite well who is to be sampled and how, the respondents will find loopholes and ambiguities that you never anticipated. For example, the directions to teachers on the California Assessment Program say: "Limited English Proficient students who are not instructed with grade level materials are exempt from testing." We received numerous questions about that direction: What about LEP students who clearly can't read but who are instructed with grade-level materials in a "sheltered English" situation? What about students who are reading materials designated for the grade level but who are at the low end of the difficulty level? What about the LEP students who are placed in regular classes because there are no special programs available but who can't really understand what's happening? Whenever possible, have a teacher, preferably your most contentious, read data collection directions and identify ambiguities.

Thoroughly orient and train data collectors.

Too many of us give a cursory glance at test/questionnaire directions and think, "Oh, this is just like last year." Those who don't give a cursory glance wait until administration time to read directions. If teachers are administering some "standardized" task—an essay, a group discussion, or even a state-mandated test—it is wise to go through a simulated administration prior to data collection, having some participants role-playing unruly or inattentive students, to point out administration procedures that are tricky, ambiguous, or in need of special attention. You'd be surprised, for example, at how many teachers cannot answer student questions about how much time is allotted for testing, or whether guessing is encouraged/allowed, or whether they should write in pen or pencil. If you are collecting information that will be machine scored and students must be provided codes for their language status, identification numbers, or the like, it is crucial to get this information to teachers well in advance and to remind them to check student answer sheets for accuracy.

If data collection involves observations, essays, student performances or products, or extended interviews, the data collectors need to know the conditions under which each is to be collected. Should all class observations occur during the morning when "skills" are taught? Should teachers be told in advance that the observers are coming? Are students allowed any assistance while producing essays, projects, or performances? Are dictionaries allowed? Calculators? Cue cards? What are the time limits? Should students have names or just identification numbers? Ask yourself what variables other than the program could explain performance differences among classrooms and try to eliminate as many as are realistic through standardized conditions. Use administrators who fully understand and will enforce those conditions.

Many observations and open-ended interviews, furthermore, require data collectors to be extensively trained—to make sure they understand their tasks as well as how to code and follow up on particular responses and how to reliably and consistently use given instruments. Training in these cases requires thorough orientation to the purposes of the instrument, the meaning of its questions or categories, illustrations, and practical examples of applying the instrument, as well as plenty of practice, and actually a final test to verify that the data collectors know how to appropriately and correctly use the instrument.

Motivate respondents when necessary.

If you want the information you gather to be useful, you must organize and think though your data collection effort well in advance of actually administering instruments. Because people at the school level are not always highly motivated to take time out of a busy schedule to respond to questionnaires or interviews, you will need to prepare a convincing statement of the importance of respondent participation in the data collection effort. We have found that explaining the purpose of a teacher questionnaire at a brief faculty meeting, then providing time for teachers to respond and return their questionnaires on the spot, has resulted in a better return rate.

To increase parent survey response, some principals reward classrooms that have 90% return by allowing students first place in the lunch line or a free ice cream much as has been done during PTA membership drives. Collecting data from small children (grades K-3) generally involves no more motivating than to say, "We would like . . ., please do your best." When tasks might be difficult for young children, they need to be reassured that the task is indeed difficult and that they are doing well.

Middle and high school students often take data collection more seriously when a researcher visits and asks for their cooperation (and candid opinions); it would appear that the presence of an authoritative outsider sometimes invokes "company" behavior. Depending upon the situation at your school, student council members could ask students to complete surveys. Achievement and attitude measures that could raise student anxiety or that are logically part of the instructional sequence are best administered by the teacher.

Better yet are evaluative devices that are built into instruction such as journals, logs, writing pieces, or group discussions that ask students to reflect upon what they have learned, how they are learning, what difficulties they are having in a particular area, and what their triumphs are. Monitoring these assignments periodically will provide important feedback for program improvement and for tracking the development of independent learners.

Monitor return rates and follow up.

And, when other approaches fail, persistence pays off. Plan to set up tracking systems to monitor carefully what data are received and what are still outstanding, instrument by instrument. Then, follow up, follow up, follow up. If your first request for information does not yield a response, send out a second, even a third, and fourth request. Your persistence communicates the importance of the effort (and may enhance "guilt" responses). You want return rates as close to 100% as possible. Otherwise, you don't know whether your responses really reflect the population, or whether they reflect mostly the complainers, the pollyannas, or what.

Anticipate potential snags.

As "data day" approaches, review your management plan and be sure that materials and procedures are in order. If this is your first experience in planning a comprehensive evaluation, review the time lines associated with using various kinds of measures (Table 3.2) and say to yourself, "If anything can go wrong, it will." We have run into and created our share of data collection disasters. Perhaps a list of some of our more important oversights will help you cut your own losses. These disasters include

- forgetting to ask students to put their names on questionnaires and tests, which made it impossible for us to match student attitudes with achievement;
- ordering the wrong version of a primary grade battery, a version that did not include the subtest we needed to gather information about LEP student language use;

- not double-checking our test inventory and running short of answer sheets, causing us to Xerox extras and then later transfer student responses, by hand, to the machine-scorable sheets;
- scheduling data collection for the day after Halloween and the day before Memorial Day;
- supervising a teacher committee developing an algebra screening exam under such highly politicized circumstances that items could not be revised even though data indicated they were poor; and
- not reading test administration directions far enough in advance to be able to answer teacher questions in time for administering the test.

When all else fails, call for help.

On the other hand, we have avoided many problems by making quick calls to friends at other schools for advice, for a rundown of the instrument administration procedures, or for extra materials. We have even called our friends in the state's Department of Education to deal with problems arising during administration of state tests. And we have memorized the test publisher's 800 number for requesting an overnight shipment of test materials (although this strategy works best when you're in the same time zone).

Suggested Readings

As important as knowing the nuts and bolts of instrument development and data collection is a grasp of the reasons why certain procedures are important. Thus a knowledge of how data collection designs reduce competing explanations for your findings and strategies for making evaluation plans are useful.

Fitz-Gibbon, C. T., & Morris, L. L. (1987). *How to design a program evaluation.* Newbury Park, CA: Sage.
If you like the thought of countering alternative explanations for any evaluation findings you unearth, this is the book for you. It describes sampling methods and research designs (data collection methods) that allow you to determine just which effects you can attribute to your program as opposed to one-time favorable circumstances (such as "the students were smart.").

Herman, J. L., Morris, L. L., & Fitz-Gibbon, C. T. (1987). *Evaluator's handbook.* Newbury Park, CA: Sage.
A book providing the "big picture" for those in a hurry. Flowcharts, summaries, and bulleted information lead the administrator through evaluation models and the steps involved in each aspect of evaluation. The model evaluation report and the checklist format make this indispensable for the administrator hiring an evaluation consultant.

King, J. A., Morris, L. L., & Fitz-Gibbon, C. T. (1987). *How to assess program implementation.* Newbury Park, CA: Sage.
This kit hits the mark for school-based evaluation with three chapters on data collection, including such topics as how to plan, how to get information from existing records, questionnaires, interviews, and observation. It is clear and applicable in the school setting.

Stecher, B. M., & Davis, W. A. (1987). *How to focus an evaluation.* Newbury Park, CA: Sage.
Already mentioned earlier, the chapter on how to formulate an evaluation plan comes in useful now. It is especially helpful when you've hired a consultant and want to know what to ask.

4

Step Four
Scoring and Summarizing Data

Overview

Your task in Step Four is to score the achievement and attitude measures used in your evaluation and to summarize these scores in a way that will enable you to answer your evaluation questions. In this step, you will also summarize and organize archival data such as attendance records, counseling referrals, or grade point average reports.

What You Should Know Before Scoring

Multiple choice and selected response scores.

As we move toward using performance assessments to measure curriculum goals and school quality, the scoring process becomes an important step in establishing both the meaning of a measure and its validity. With multiple choice or selected response measures, for instance, where for each item students choose from among given alternatives or where respondents indicate their response on a numerical scale, the *score* is simply the number of correct items or the frequency of respondents selecting a certain response choice. Scoring means simply "counting" the number of correct answers as determined by a preestablished answer key. We know what the scores *mean* on selected response and multiple choice measures by looking at the items and the knowledge/skill framework those items are supposed to represent. For example, a score of 8 on a 10-item calculus quiz assessing the concept of integration suggests that the student understood the concept pretty well (as measured by this particular set of 10 items). Or a score on a questionnaire where 90% of parent respondents selected "agree" or "very much agree" on the item "my child is happy in school" means nearly all parents answering the questionnaire felt that their children were happy in school. The score meaning in both examples was determined prior to the administration of the measure, at the time when the conceptual framework for the assessment was established (often called a *content-process matrix* in achievement test design) and when the items and their prespecified alternatives were written.

For multiple choice or selected response measures, the test's conceptual framework predetermines what "knowledge of calculus" or what "a good school" means, what the questions assessing them will be, and what the range of answer choices will be. Respondents react to given choices, and, in traditional multiple choice tests, their responses are either right or wrong, with nothing in between.

Performance assessment scores.

Although score meaning for performance assessments, essays, portfolios, projects, demonstrations, and the like is also a function of the kinds of questions asked and the expected responses, respondents are not given preestablished answers. As with selected response measures, performance assessments are grounded in a conceptual framework that defines the nature of the task or the nature of the questions students are asked to complete. It also defines the types or range of tasks that constitute good writing, scientific problem solving, social studies understanding, everyday math applications, and so on—but we can't anticipate in advance the entire range of possible answers. Thus the *process* of reviewing and judging answers to open-ended tasks (what we call "scoring" here) determines the score meaning as much as the initial tasks themselves. Scoring, for performance assessments, means using a set of criteria to rate the quality of students' responses.

The scoring criteria, often called *rubrics,* define the essential features of a quality response; they enable us to attach standardized meaning to students' performance, almost always along a continuum of quality. Although not all would agree that scoring criteria should be created before a performance test is administered, we strongly feel that, because such tests are being used at the school level to focus instruction and to assess school quality and student performance, fairness demands that expectations be public and known in advance. Teachers and students need to know what is expected of them, and therefore at least a draft set of criteria should exist prior to test administration. These criteria, scoring guidelines, or rubrics, represent our best guesses (or best theory) of what reasonable continua of performance are, from novice or unskilled to highly expert, or what constitutes different levels of understanding of a particular topic/concept or field.

Although our scoring criteria reflect our preconceptions of what the nature of a correct response is, much as the response alternatives in a good multiple choice test do, the difference is that, with performance assessment, the scoring criteria may be altered and adapted to reflect unanticipated or novel answers, and answers are rated on a continuum of quality. Thus scoring becomes more than a matter of counting and checking against an answer key. For performance assessments, scoring means judging the quality of a response in comparison with prespecified criteria (or a draft version of such criteria) and rating a response along a continuum (or, more often, continua) of possible responses.

Outside versus local scoring.

The practical implication of this distinction between scoring a selected response versus scoring a constructed response measure is that you will need to think of scoring differently for different types of instruments. For selected response instruments, hand scoring with an answer key or machine scoring either locally or by a test publisher is an easily managed and easily automated process that will not involve staff time in any substantial way. With performance assessments and with open-ended interview or questionnaire responses, however, the scoring process is also part of the process by which we understand what the scores and their underlying responses mean. To derive the greatest benefits from using these kinds of measures, you will want to involve in scoring the staff members who will be most involved with using the results. If, for example, you are having students compile science portfolios, you would want the science department to develop (or adapt from existing models) scoring criteria that they agree are meaningful and suitable and then actually to score the portfolios. This way, members of your science department would be able to see the range of student performance and to understand how their particular students understand science as it is taught in your school.

Although some test publishers offer off-site scoring services for writing samples, and no doubt will eventually do so for other types of performance assessments, if you use this service, you will lose the opportunity to involve your teachers in a review of both your student essays and the scoring guidelines. This review helps teachers come to a consensus about how student work should be judged, standardizes their judgments, and often carries over into instruction. We have seen this happen in high school English departments, after teachers work together to score a set of grade-12 essays using the California Assessment Program rubrics. They apply those same rubrics in their own classrooms for peer review and for grading students. Similarly, we have seen teachers involved in the development and scoring of district writing assessments bring improved focus to their writing instruction and use the scoring scheme to provide efficient feedback to students on their classroom writing. Over time, this produced improvement in students' writing performance.

Different scores, different uses.

Prior to the scoring process, you will need to think about the kind of score that will be most useful in answering your evaluation questions. There are a variety of different types of scores, and each has specific uses and limitations. Examples follow:

- If you need to compare scores between different assessments that are supposed to measure the same things but with different numbers of items or different difficulty levels, you will need to use some type of derived score (percentile rank, standard score, scale score, normal curve equivalent, stanine) rather than the number-correct or raw score.
- If you want to compare across different kinds of measures, you might use a derived score such as the percentage of students at the success or effectiveness level you designated in Step Two.
- Questionnaire results typically are summarized as the percentage of respondents choosing each alternative (or the percentage within a range) or as the mean item score (an average over the item scale).
- Writing samples and many performance assessments often are summarized as a mean (average) quality rating or as the percentage of students scoring at or above some designated quality rating.

Table 4.1 summarizes the most commonly used scores.

Total score or subscale score?

In addition to the type of score you will use, you will be faced with choice in the level of detail you wish to report. Most standardized tests report total scores in each area assessed: typically, reading, language, and mathematics. Within these content areas, subtest scores for specific strands of skills also are provided, such as for vocabulary, math concepts, applications, and so on. The total score gives a general picture of performance and has the advantage of being more stable or consistent than subtest scores. Subtest scores, on the other hand, provide more diagnostic detail and help pinpoint areas of strength and weakness.

Questionnaire's scores also are often reported in subscales—a set of questions measuring different aspects of the same topic, such as parent satisfaction with the school program, teacher expectations for student performance, or staff satisfaction with school policies. Responses to individual items then help to identify areas of relative strength and weakness with regard to the subscale area assessed.

TABLE 4.1 Summary of Score Types by Instrument

Nationally normed standardized tests
Raw score: number correct
Individual pupil percentile rank: percentage of students scoring at or below given score
School/district percentile rank: percentage of schools/districts scoring at or below given score
Stanine: section of the normal distribution into which score falls; 1 = lowest and 9 = highest
Normal curve equivalent: transformed percentile rank to create equal interval scale; used for Chapter 1 reporting
Scale/standard score: transformed score on arbitrary scale such as SAT scores

Selected resonse curriculum-related tests (including minimum competency)
Raw score: number correct
Percentage correct: number correct over total possible points

Selected response questionnaires
Frequency: actual number of people choosing a particular response alternative for a particular item
Proportion/percentage: response frequencies converted into percentages for comparison purposes

Performance tests
Raw score: rating assigned to a paper/performance/portfolio by a judge based on a set of scoring criteria

Archival data
Frequencies: number of students in scoring categories such as "10-15 absences"
Proportions/percentages: frequencies converted into percentages for comparison purposes

The question of whether to use a total score or a subscale score becomes a little more complex when it comes to performance assessments. Although many writing assessments use only one holistic rubric and report a single overall score, you also will find numerous writing assessments that score essays on a number of analytic scales, using rubrics such as "organization," "content," "support," "style," "mechanics." You will need to decide whether you want a summary of performance or a profile that can provide more diagnostic, instructionally relevant information.

Similar decisions need to be made in assessing complex performances that incorporate a variety of behaviors and content, such as projects or portfolios. An overall total score may suit your needs, representing an overall impression much as the holistic essay score summarizes a variety of qualities, or you may use subscales scores, each representing different dimensions of performance.

If you are tracking your school's progress over time, an overall impression or total score can simplify the task. When you are interested program improvement, however, the profiles of student performance across different dimensions will be very useful.

Selecting Scoring Procedures

In this section, we suggest useful scoring procedures for the most commonly used evaluation measures beginning with the most traditional, norm-referenced, standardized tests, and concluding with the newest, performance and portfolio assessments.

Published tests. For published standardized, norm-referenced multiple choice achievement tests and attitude surveys, you need only return the answer documents to the publisher, request scores and score reports, and await your results. We suggest that, in addition to percentile ranks, you request a raw score and a normal curve equivalent or standard score.

The percentile ranks will be useful for reporting results to parents and teachers, but the raw scores will help both to understand the absolute performance. For example, a parent once called, distraught that her 99th percentile student received an 85th percentile rank in grade-3 vocabulary. A look at the raw score reported with the ranking showed that, of 20 items on the test, the student missed only 3. The parent was relieved about her student's performance and enlightened about the "real" meaning of percentile ranks. You will need normal curve equivalent (NCE) scores for reporting test results for state and federally funded programs such as Chapter 1 or Title VII. These scores are useful for calculating averages, graphing results over time, and making comparisons between different groups. The standard score can be used for the same purposes as the NCE, but, because each test publisher calculates standard scores differently, these are not as useful for making comparisons between different tests.

Your school district may have the equipment and the license for in-house scoring of published tests. In that case, you can ask the district data processing director to produce raw, percentile, and NCE scores. Although in-house scoring is quick and cheap, we have found that errors can creep into the test scoring and summarizing process. You will need to review the kinds of reports available and determine how summary scores are calculated. The most frequent mistakes we've seen are averaged percentile ranks (because percentile scores are not an equal interval scale, they cannot be averaged) and percentile ranks graphed on an equal-interval scale. We've also seen the mean score used to designate the 50th percentile rank instead of the median, which is not a serious error if your scores are normally distributed but can be quite a distortion if you have a very high- or very low-achieving population.

If some of your measures are scored by a publisher or at the district, you will be ordering score reports or summaries as well as specifying how scores are to be reported back. For program evaluation purposes, in addition to the usual class- and grade-level alpha lists of student results, you will want frequency distributions by class and grade level for each subtest. You may want your frequency distributions to specify the number and percentage of students scoring in each stanine or quartile, depending upon whether you need to look closely at the percentage of students scoring in the extremes of a distribution. You will also want to order a "criterion-referenced" analysis that displays the percentage of students correctly answering the cluster of items measuring a single objective. An item analysis showing the percentage of students answering each item correctly can help identify which items measure skills not taught or those that have difficult formats. Ideally, all of these reports can break down results by subgroups, such as boys and girls, limited and fluent English proficient, or students in the school for two years or more versus those new to the school. Score summaries by class and grade level and subgroup results by grade level form the "stuff" of your evaluation.

School-developed selected response questionnaires.

Every evaluation incorporates locally developed measures, many of which use "Scan-tron" technology for summarizing results. The majority of items on most teacher, student, and parent questionnaires ask respondents to indicate their response on some numerical scale (e.g., a five-point Likert scale of agree to disagree), either by circling their response or by marking their choice on a Scan-tron or optical-scan score sheet. You should know that special answer sheets can be purchased to enable you to score questionnaire items using your test-scoring Scan-tron equipment. With these special sheets, the scanner tallies the frequency of each answer choice, "a" to "e," for each item. When you push the button to get a "read out," instead of getting the number of students answering an item incorrectly (the usual Scan-tron read out), you get the number of respondents picking 1a, 1b, 1c, and so on. If you copy this information and transfer it to a spreadsheet, you can easily calculate the percentage of people selecting each rating, 1 to 5, for each item, which then essentially becomes your questionnaire score. Scan-trons also supply Apple and IBM compatible software to fully automate the scoring of both tests and questionnaires. The software allows you to produce the kinds of summary reports you will need to analyze your evaluation information.

If your data processing department has optical-scanning equipment and the time to program software to score your selected response questionnaire, you will use optical-scan answer sheets. The sheets are read by the district computer and a report summarizing the number and percentage of people choosing each response for each question is generated by the software program.

When you have only a small number of surveys, perhaps 30 or fewer, it is not difficult to summarize your information by hand. Set up a tally sheet with the survey question numbers and each response choice on the left-hand side. Tally the number of people selecting each response. Add up the tallies and convert the numbers into the percentage of people choosing each response. The percentages can be calculated in either of two ways: the number of people selecting "a," "b," "c," and so on, divided by the total number of people responding to that question, or the number of people selecting a response alternative divided by the total number answering the survey. You will find that not all respondents will answer all items so that it is often more accurate to calculate your response percentages using the totals for each question.

School-developed open-ended questionnaire or interview questions.

Often, your most valuable feedback comes from respondent comments or answers to open-ended questions such as this one: "In what areas do you think we could do a better job?" These responses also can be summarized and tallied. First, read through the entire set of surveys to get an overall picture of the kinds of comments being made. Then, decide upon possible categories for these comments. For example, in response to the question, "In what areas do you think we could do a better job," common answers might include

"Assign more homework."
"I think the children need better playground supervision."
"My student feels unsafe in the rest rooms."
"I don't think my student is being challenged."
"Why can't students earning a 'B' take prealgebra?"

You can see three categories emerging in the above set of comments: campus safety, course expectations, and math assignment policy. You might have labeled these categories differently, but the point is that your categories serve as a starting point to tally and summarize comments. As you attempt to fit comments into the categories you have chosen, you will probably have to refine or redefine some of them. You should have a colleague read through the surveys and try to fit the comments into your categories as a check for consistency in labeling and tallying comments. Discuss any discrepancies and adjust your scoring procedure accordingly. The score for your open-ended questions and comments will in fact be the sum of the tallies for each category emerging from the data.

When you are summarizing open-ended questions, whether from an interview, questionnaire, or student work sample, be on the lookout for anecdotes or quotations that exemplify or characterize certain viewpoints or kinds of work. These examples will help illuminate your numerical summaries and clarify points of view encountered during your evaluation.

Observations.

Scoring observations will depend upon the observation strategy used. For an observation checklist or one that uses a structured, selected response format, simply tally and total the number of times each category was observed, much as was done with survey responses.

The score for a scripted or narrative observation is obtained in the same way as the score for open-ended survey responses. You and a colleague can read through the observation scripts and identify descriptors or categories for the behaviors noted. Have someone tally recurring behaviors or classroom characteristics, and then check your categories and tallies by having another colleague go through the process. The observation score, like the score for open-ended survey or interview questions, will be the percentage of tallies falling into each category.

School-developed writing samples and other performance measures.

Scoring writing samples entails three basic steps: (a) developing or adapting scoring criteria, (b) training scorers, and (c) holding a scoring session where you randomly assign papers to scorers and use procedures to assure reliability. Other types of performance assessment also require these same general steps.

Although description of the details of each of these tasks is beyond the scope of this book, you might refer to a recent CRESST publication, *Cognitively Sensitive Assessments of Student Writing in Content Areas* (Baker, Aschbacher, Niemi, & Yamaguchi, 1991), for more specific guidelines. Some general information to keep in mind follows:

- Definition of scoring criteria is a critical issue. Ideally, you will at least have a preliminary set of scoring criteria in mind when you draft your essay questions or performance tasks. Be aware that there are a number of models that can be adapted to your situation (and the number is growing rapidly as more states, districts, and others explore alternative student assessments).
- Consider developing or adapting scoring rubrics that can be applicable in more than one content area. For example, the CRESST rubrics developed by Baker et al. to score content understanding in social studies essays include "use of principles," "evidence of misconceptions," and "content quality." The rubrics also have been used to score science and math explanations.
- The training and scoring session can be held on the same day. Involve teachers at the same grade level or of the same subject so that consensus on scoring guidelines will not be difficult to reach.

- You will need to decide whether an overall score will be assigned to each piece or whether you will have subscores for different dimensions such as content, style, and support.
- You will need to decide whether papers will be read by two or more readers (the recommended practice) or whether you will use some other procedures to assure the reliability of ratings. If you use two or more readers, plan to report an average score on each paper or to total the ratings.

Portfolios and complex projects and performances.

The scores from portfolios or from complex performances such as dance, drama, or art and student projects, can be extremely useful for program evaluation. The issues you consider are similar to those in scoring writing assessments.

When scoring complex performances, you will have to consider whether one score is sufficient to describe student work or whether several unique scores are needed. For example, the Vermont mathematics portfolios require that portfolios include five to seven samples of student work and are scored on seven different dimensions, using a four-point scale of quality for each dimension, such as evidence of task understanding, reflection, analysis, language of mathematics, and clarity. The seven dimensions are summarized in two major scores, one for problem solving and one for communication.

For program evaluation purposes, multiple scores such as those used in Vermont could be reported in a variety of ways: You could look at the average scores for each of the seven scoring categories. You could, as did Vermont, aggregate the categories into two major categories, problem solving and communication, then average the scores for these two areas. Or you could calculate some kind of overall score.

Score Summaries and Score Reports

The scoring process is complete when you have score reports or some type of score summary in hand for each instrument. For standardized tests, you can work with your sales representative to select the kinds of score reports most useful for answering your evaluation questions. Most often, these are some type of criterion-referenced report such as the percentage of students mastering each objective measured by the test. Another often used score summary is the report of student score distributions on each test (frequency distributions).

Your score reports for selected response portions of questionnaires will show the entire distribution of responses for each item and may include the mean (average) response. If you are aggregating items into subscales, the report will show averages or distributions for each subscale.

Reports for essays, projects, or performance tests can be handled in much the same way as those for more traditional tests. You can report the percentage of students meeting prespecified standards represented by a certain rating, such as the percentage of students scoring "5" or better on a nine-point scale. You could report scores as the average rating achieved by students or you could report the percentage of students scoring at each point of the rating scale for each dimension.

You may need to represent your score summaries in more than one way to clarify your evaluation questions. As discussed in the next step, your analyses, interpretations, and reporting will be directly guided by these questions. For example, if you asked, "Are our students meeting district standards in writing," and your district hopes that all students can be rated as "competent" or higher on the district writing scale, you could summarize your scores as the percentage of students scoring below the "competent" score point and the percentage scoring at or above that point. If, however, you are interested in knowing how to improve, you will want to know the percentage of students scoring at each level to see whether you need to work with a large population of low-scoring students or whether you need to improve in the higher ranges of the score scale.

Worksheet 4.1 provides one type of a data summary. A blank working copy appears in Resource C. Once you have your scores summarized, you are ready to answer you evaluation questions, the task in Step Five.

Suggested Readings

Most of the wisdom about scores and scoring is buried in university research or test publisher technical reports. Although an important topic to those having to manage the nuts-and-bolts aspects of scoring, scoring hardly merits a full-fledged book of its own. When it comes to developing scoring procedures and rubrics for performance tests, portfolios, and projects, be sure to avail yourself of presentations at local and national conferences for current information in this rapidly changing scene. Some recent releases we've found helpful follow.

Baker, E. L., Aschbacher, P. R., Niemi, D., & Yamaguchi, E. (1991). *Cognitively sensitive assessment of student writing in content areas.* Los Angeles: CRESST.
This document is a virtual how-to manual for training teachers to use a research-based scoring rubric designed to score high school social studies essays. It includes step-by-step guidelines for preparing training materials, getting interrater agreement, and calculating reliability. Especially useful is the comprehensive scoring rubric that was developed using the best minds in content assessment in the country. The rubric can be adapted for local use.

Sample Worksheet 4.1
Summarizing Data

Instrument	*Score Selected*	*Summary Method*
Questionnaire/Survey: Parent questionnaire items related to math program (Items 3, 6, 7, 9, 12)	Percentage Frequencies	Average percentages across categories "1-2" and "4-5" Bar graph of percentage choosing "4-5" for each item Mean choice for each question (average of choices 1-5 on each item)
Nationally Normed Test: ITBS Math Concepts and Problem Solving	Percentile rank Standard score	Line graph of median PRs for past 3 years by grade level and subtest Median percentile rank for each class and grade Distribution of percentage of students scoring in each stanine and in each quartile range Mean standard score
Selected Response Curriculum-Related Tests: Competency test: Math	Percentage-correct score	Percentage scoring above the passing standard (65%) Bar graph of percentage passing math for past 5 years
Performance Tests: State assessment: open-ended math item; Grade-8 math portfolios	Raw score (rating) Average raw score (rating)	Frequency and percentage of students receiving each rating (1-6) Frequency and percentage of average ratings across 7 papers (1-6 scale) Bar graphs comparing average ratings for girls versus boys Bar graphs comparing average ratings for LEP versus others
Interviews (open-ended responses): Interviews with 3 students in each math class	Frequency of answers classified in the same category	List of student comments arranged from most to least frequent about satisfaction with math class
Archival Information: Attendance; Course enrollment; Course grade distribution report	Raw score: number of absences in math each period Raw score: number enrolled in each math section Frequencies of grades A-F by course and section	Average number of weekly absences for weeks 2, 5, 10, 16 Line graphs of weekly absence rate for target weeks Average section enrollment by course for weeks 1, 3, 5, 20 Line graph of course enrollment across time by course, grade 8, prealgebra, algebra Average "grade" (A-F) for each math course across sections

Finch, F. (Ed.). (1991). *Educational performance assessment.* Chicago: Riverside.

Who said the appendix was a vestigial organ? The appendixes in this monograph produced by the publisher of the *Iowa Tests of Basic Skills* provide sample performance test exercises and scoring rubrics developed for the Arizona state assessment as well as sample leaders' and scorers' manuals. These documents make tangible procedures for scoring reading, writing, and mathematics performance tasks. The chapter on problems in scoring performance tests by Steve Osterland, formerly of the Oakland (California) school district and now with the University of Missouri, alerts practitioners to the problems in scoring performance tests. In sum, there are many examples, and the book is practitioner friendly.

Morris, L. L., Fitz-Gibbon, C. T., & Lindheim, E. (1987). *How to measure performance and use tests.* Newbury Park, CA: Sage.

Previously described as a resource for identifying tracking strategies, the chapter on validity and reliability of performance assessments should be read before you even think about setting up a scoring session.

5

Step Five
Analyze Information and Interpret Findings

Overview

In this step, you will review score summaries and reports with your advisory group to answer each of your evaluation questions. The focus during Step Five shifts from thinking about scores and summaries of particular measures back to the larger purpose of your evaluation: looking across those summaries to answer your specific questions. You will need Worksheet 4.1, suggested data summaries for each evaluation question, and your results to begin.

Data Interpretation: A Dialogue About Meaning

Although the first image that comes to mind when we think about analyzing data is a rather fearsome task involving numbers, scores, tables, graphs, and computer printouts, *analysis* is simply another term for a common human activity: looking for meaning, seeing relationships between parts and the whole. Your consolidated evaluation plan linking specific evaluation questions to particular measures provides a pathway for data analysis: You group score summaries and information by evaluation question, then examine what answers emerge by looking at results relative to the standards you specified, by looking at trends over time, and/or by looking for relationships between program processes and outcomes for reporting.

Involve others in data interpretation.

Data summaries and sophisticated analyses cannot direct an agenda for action. Data can raise issues for consideration among knowledgeable stakeholders. Data can supplement, but not supplant, our working knowledge. Data can stimulate thoughtful discussion about the nature of the challenges faced by the school and the progress it is making toward meeting those challenges.

In short, the interpretation of evaluation data not only is a technical task but needs to be seen as part of the problem-solving, decision-making process of the school. Discussion of systematically gathered and summarized information can be an effective management technique for building consensus about school goals and success if it involves key constituencies. These constituencies will help you generate the meanings and implications of the data you have collected, strengthening the support for change. The inclusion of teacher, parent, student, or community groups in reviewing data, furthermore, permits a richer interpretation of the findings and can help provide explanations for results.

A good strategy for traversing Step Five, then, is to provide your steering committee with the relevant data summaries—tables, graphs, survey summaries, and so on—bearing on each evaluation question. Ask members to review data related to each question and to speculate on the meaning of the results: What answers do they suggest? Have a member of the committee summarize the group responses. As you review the information, resolve discrepancies in interpretations, make a note of information that is incomplete or of places where you would like more information, and generate possible explanations suggested by the data or by your steering committee.

The goal of data interpretation is to identify what courses of action would be most likely to help you meet your school goals. What changes in activities should be made? What kind of staff in-service is needed? What additional resources are needed? Should parent or community involvement be widened? For example, if our answer to the question, "How are we doing in math?" is "pretty well on the average but not so well for LEP students," then we will want to strengthen our program for these latter students. Perhaps the teachers on the advisory committee will suggest that they would like more help providing sheltered instruction to LEP students. Other suggestions could relate to a peer tutoring program and a bilingual parent evening where parents are shown how to help students in math using their native language.

Certainly, the answers to all of your questions will not be found in tables of average test scores for different groups of students, graphs of responses comparing student-parent-teacher responses to similar questions on surveys, or notes from classroom observations. But hypotheses or suggestions derived from these data can initiate discussion among the "experts" you have selected to help you review the data. The discussions will validate some findings, will provide explanations for others, and also can help to uncover areas where findings are invalid.

Although the evaluation questions for your school will be more specific than the ones we have used in this guide, the strategies for reviewing and interpreting data to answering certain kinds of questions will be the same. Below, we suggest strategies for organizing and analyzing your data by question and then provide illustrations for needs assessment and formative evaluation questions.

Organize Your Data by Question

One of the most common mistakes made in data analysis is getting mired in the numbers and losing sight of the goal, which is to answer your evaluation questions. You easily can get so engrossed in the results of a single instrument, such as a standardized test or a teacher questionnaire, that attention shifts from answering a question to analyzing a particular set of scores. You spent a lot of time designing your evaluation so that you would have multiple measures to inform each question and to corroborate your findings: Stick to this focus!

Therefore, while it may be easier and more efficient for you to prepare summaries instrument by instrument, resist the temptation. It will be much easier for your committee to synthesize information from multiple data sources if you only provide them with those results and score summaries related to a particular evaluation question. Table 5.1 provides an example of a data display using multiple sources but edited to address only one evaluation question.

Remember the basic building blocks of data analysis.

Your data summaries by evaluation question will draw on the same score summaries that were presented in the last chapter. These included such summary statistics as means, medians, modes, and distributions (frequency of responses or number of students at particular score points). Standard deviations and correlation coefficients, furthermore, are routine products of computerized score summaries and will be useful when answering questions about relationships or in comparing two or more score distributions. If you have forgotten some or most of the uses of these building blocks from your "Stat. 101" class, the Suggested Readings at the end of this step provides several clearly written, practitioner-relevant sources you can use for references in preparing to analyze data. We also would like to add that this is one place you might want to call in an expert for help in selecting appropriate statistics and preparing clear data summaries. The expert can also review your questions and evaluation design and determine whether more complicated and sophisticated analyses such as significance testing are appropriate.

TABLE 5.1 Sample Data Organized by Evauation Question

Question 1: How are our students doing in math at grade 8?

State math test	*1991*	*1990*
Concepts	213	200
Problems	245	212
Computation	200	200

ITBS subtest	*1991*	*1990*[*]	*1989*
Concepts	69 median PR	54 median PR	73 median PR
Problem Solving	73 median PR	60 median PR	63 median PR

[*] Norms change

Parent Survey Responses to Statement: My child can complete math homework without assistance (95% response rate)

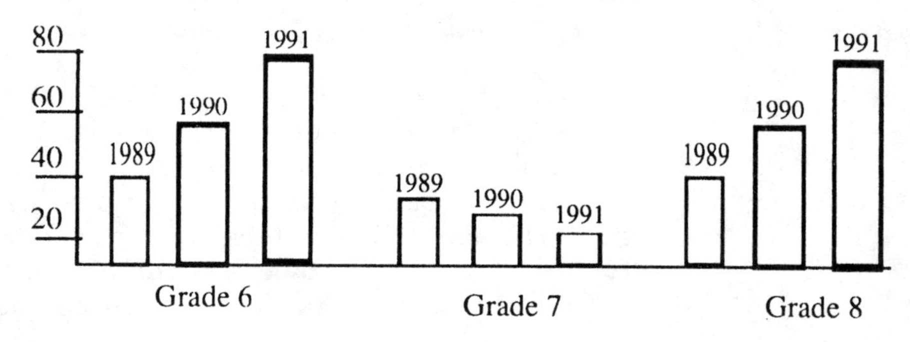

Comparison of Coastal Village Intermediate Math Scores with East Coast Intermediate and Gulf Coast Intermediate Schools: ITBS Problem Solving, 1991

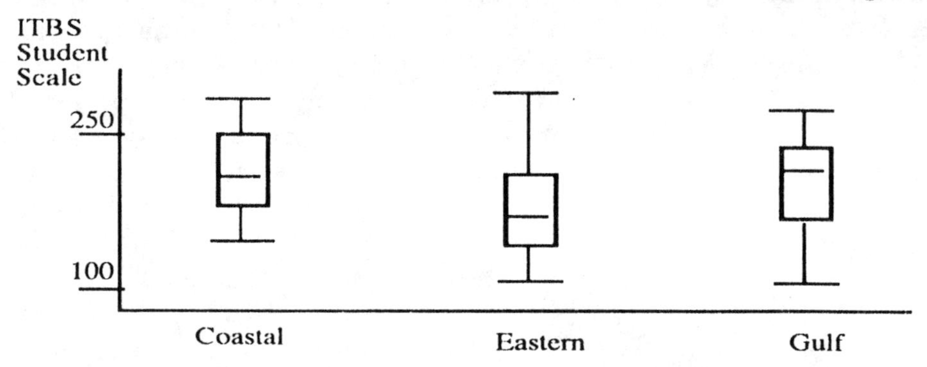

Remember that you have several options in displaying data.

In presenting data summaries to your committee, be aware that we all have different preferred ways of looking at information; some of us prefer numbers, but many of us can see things more clearly through graphs and pictures.

There are any number of formats for presenting your data. You can use tables to present frequency distributions or summary statistics

TABLE 5.2 Ideal Formats for Displaying Information

- Bar graphs are best for static comparisons and comparing unlike kinds of information. Plain "vanilla" bar charts help people make more accurate comparisons than pie charts, stacked bar charts, or three dimensional bar charts.
  - —Test results for one year
  - —Comparison of reading and mathematics results
  - —Percentage of people responding "Very Satisfied" to different questions on a survey
  - —Comparison of reading scores at different schools
- Line graphs are best for presenting trends. A single representation with multiple graph lines is better for representing multiple trends than several separate graphs.
  - —Reading and mathematics scores from 1985 to 1988
  - —Percentage of LEP students since 1984 for the state, district, and school
  - —Trends in percentage of budget spent on certain categories such as salaries, supplies, security
- Pie charts are best for showing part-whole relationships.
  - —Percentage of LEP, FEP, English-speaking students
  - —Percentage of budget spent on various categories
  - —Percentage of teachers holding emergency credentials
- Pictographs provide rapid general impressions.
  - —A graph composed of "happy faces" showing student attitude toward reading and mathematics
  - —A bar graph of dollar signs showing how utility costs have climbed since 1980
- Tables are best for providing exact numbers, but they are less likely to be read or understood than graphs.

for several instruments in a compact format. You can use frequency polygons (line graphs) to show trends over time. Bar graphs (histograms) are useful in comparing percentages and average scores on the same scale for different instruments, such as the math concepts and problem-solving tests. Table 5.2 presents some rules of thumb for displaying different kinds of data. If you incorporate these guidelines with those presented in Table 5.3, which summarizes the research on effective data display, you'll have no problem deciding how to prepare your data summaries.

TABLE 5.3 Guidelines for Creating Effective Graphs and Tables

General Guidelines

- Do not write heading in all capitals. Use both upper and lower case.
- Sentences worded negatively are stronger than those worded positively. These are best used to present information that is contrary to a reader's expectations. Because negatively worded sentences are more difficult to understand and are so emphatic, use them sparingly.
- Questions at the beginning of textual explanations help readers focus on and remember important information.
- Color coded bars and lines on graphs help readers compare information more easily than lines and bars in the same color.

Bar Charts

- Information should be labeled directly on the chart rather than through a "key" or "legend."
- Horizontal bar charts leave more room for labels but may be more difficult to read.

Line Graphs

- Avoid clutter, both of lines and tic marks.
- Choose the range of tic marks to include the entire range of the data; avoid scale breaks.
- If scale breaks are necessary, do not connect numerical values on either side of a break.
- Choose a scale so that data fill up as much of the region as possible.
- Zero does not always have to be included in a scale.
- Use a logarithmic scale when presenting multiplicative factors.

Pictographs

- Symbols should be self-explanatory and easily differentiated from one another.
- Quantity is better represented by increasing the number rather than the size of symbols.

Tables

- Round numbers to no more than two significant digits.
- Provide row and column averages.
- Use columns to display the most important comparisons.
- Order rows and columns by size of numbers rather than alphabetical order.
- Set rows and columns compactly, so that the eye can make easy comparisons, rather than spacing them out across the page.

Use sensible data analysis strategies.

Multiple is a key concept throughout this guide. We tell you to use multiple data sources to answer each question and advise you to use a variety of strategies to summarize the same data. The multiple exhortation becomes especially important during data analysis and interpretation because the use of multiple analysis strategies with multiple measures enables you to substantiate your findings. The five strategies we invoke automatically in addressing evaluation questions are as follows:

- Look at trends over time.
- Compare results with a similar group or an appropriate norm group.
- Compare results against a standard.
- Monitor the performance of subgroups.
- Look for relationships between process and outcomes.

Once your have your data summaries and analyses organized so that they address each question, you are ready to close in on the answers about your school's success.

Keep in mind, however, that the data analysis process is multidimensional. You will be answering questions, entertaining explanations, hypothesizing relationships among program components, and suggesting actions for program improvement all in the same session, which is why a linear sequence of steps such as those we have presented here can be a bit misleading. In fact, as you implement sensible evaluation strategies in your school, you will find that many of the tasks in Steps Four through Six overlap and occur simultaneously.

A note on the significance of your findings.

As you examine scores over time or when you make comparisons between groups or between your school and others, you will want to know: "Is the difference I see significant?" This concept of significance has at least two meanings: important and not simply a score fluctuation within the realm of chance. Before you can determine whether a score change (or even a difference in the percentage of responses to a survey item from one year to the next) is big enough to reflect significant (important) progress, you will need tests of statistical significance; these will tell you whether the change or difference you observe is one you could expect simply because of the amount of measurement error from one occasion to the next or whether the change is larger than the natural fluctuation associated with the measurement of human performance. Only if you find that your changes over time or differences between scores are statistically significant will you be able to say that they might reflect real educational change.

Under some circumstances, rarely encountered at the school level, the difference between two scores can be statistically significant without reflecting any practical difference. Sample size is one factor that influences statistical analyses. When samples are large (more than 100), you don't need a very large difference between two scores for the difference to be labeled "statistically significant." For example, if 1,000 students take a standardized reading test in 1990 and get an average standard score of 283, and then the same group scores 288 in 1991, the difference is likely to be found to be statistically significant. In examining the number of items answered correctly, however, we may find that, on the average in 1990, the number correct was 24 out of 30 and in 1991 it was 24.7 out of 30. To most of us, this difference has no real practical impact, nor would we likely notice a marked difference in student classroom performance.

Although you will not likely be running significance tests on your own data, there will be occasions where you may want an expert to determine whether differences you've found—over time or when comparing two schools, scores, groups, or the like—reflect real differences in your program or represent expected score fluctuation due to measurement error. What you should know is that, unless these differences are statistically significant, you probably (not definitely) have no difference of any educational importance. On the other hand, when your results indicate that the difference over time or between two groups is statistically significant, you *still* aren't sure whether it is practically significant. You must exercise your own judgment by referring back to the actual performance being measured and what that score difference represents in terms of that performance before you can assert that "we have made real, practical, visible, measurable educational progress."

Answering Needs Assessment Questions

Look at findings in terms of prespecified criteria.

A needs assessment looks across the range of programs operating in your school and identifies strengths and weaknesses. Because you must make some kind of judgment of success with a needs assessment, the most direct strategy for answering the "how are we doing" or "in what areas are we in need of improvement" questions is to measure your progress against a standard or criterion. If you have not already set standards against which you wish to measure your progress because you had no "feel" for what defensible progress might be or because you were using extant data summaries prepared for other purposes, now is the time to think about which standards represent success for your school. For norm-referenced, standardized tests of various types from multiple choice to the essay-based advanced placement examinations, you could measure your success in some of the following ways:

- Compare student test results with national or state norms.
- Compare student test results with similar schools' performance.
- Look at the percentage of students scoring above the 75th percentile, at the 50th percentile, and below the 25th percentile.
- Look at the percentage of students scoring at predesignated "mastery" levels.
- Look at the percentage attaining "passing" or attaining preset standards on state honors or regents examinations, advanced placement tests, or international baccalaureate results.
- Compare current dropout rates, average daily attendance, and percentage of unexcused absences with state goals.

Table 5.4 displays data and compares results with prespecified standards for a middle school mathematics program. The table demonstrates how your method of setting standards will be determined by the kind of instrument you use. You can also see that, even though you may begin looking at your data to answer the "how are we doing" question, your analysis will lead you to consider simultaneously other issues such as "why did we not meet our goal?" and "how can we improve?" Once these questions have been raised in a discussion of findings, suggested actions for improving the program are not far behind.

Look at trends over time.

A one-year snapshot of student performance does not provide a large enough picture of your school. Did performance on key indicators such as attendance, dropouts, and grade point averages improve? Was this due to changes in the size and diversity of your student population or was it simply a one-year aberration? By looking at these same indicators for the past three to five years, you're in a better position to know whether the improvement is part of a trend. If this is your first year collecting information, you now have a baseline against which to compare future progress. Do not be too hasty in making judgments about school needs with only one year's worth of information. If this is the second or third year of progress tracking, see if the data reveal an improvement.

Look for educationally significant changes in performance. How large a change must be to reflect a practical difference will depend upon the measure you use and what kinds of performance a score change of a particular amount represents. Although some fluctuation in performance is expected each year simply due to differences in student population, is the general trend upward? Is your general trend downward, upward, or relatively stable and similar to schools

TABLE 5.4 Using Prespecified Standards to Interpret Data

Instrument	*Standard*	*Percentage Meeting*	*Conclusion*
ITBS math	50% above 50th PR	61% above 50th	Above goal: success
State assessment	Fewer in bottom quartile than last year	Bottom quartile only 8% this year; 15% last year; never lower than 13%	Met goal: success
Math competency	Fewer fails than last year	Fails: 35%; last year, 37%	About the same; goal not met
Open-ended math question	At least 50% scoring "acceptable" or above	52% scored acceptable, but only 20% of the girls did	Met goal overall but need to examine girls' performance
Grade-8 portfolios	Average rating: 4 out of 6	20% were rated 4 out of 6 or higher	Problem here; let's look more closely when we examine other data
Parent survey	At least 80% register satisfaction (rate 4-5) with new program	90% said they were happy with the program at grades 6 and 8 but only 70% at grade 7	Met goal success in grades 6, 8; let's look more closely at program in grade 7
Course enrollment	No more than 1% leave algebra for lower-level math	Algebra 1 transfer rate 30%	Problem here: Standard unrealistic? Kids not prepared? Teachers unrealistic?
Course grade distribution	At least 95% of students get "C" or higher	89% received "C" or higher, but only 75% of girls did	Close to goal: Did we set standard too high? Look at girls' performance

representing similar programs and populations? Your answers to these questions will point to school-level strengths or weaknesses in particular areas.

Table 5.1 displayed parent responses about homework over a three-year period. We can see that the percentage of parents responding that their children could complete their mathematics homework without assistance increased steadily in grades 6 and 8 over the three years, while grade 7 has the opposite trend. Even though we have not tested for significant increases over time, if the parent response rate was nearly the same over the three years and the kinds of parents returning surveys were similar to those not completing the surveys, then we can suggest that the new program has possible benefits at two grade levels. Table 5.1 also displays test score data over time. We see that scores have gone up in math concepts and problems, but not in computation, on the state assessment and the ITBS for the past two years. This information, if corroborated, indicates successful program implementation.

Before you decide that you have a certifiable success or a real problem, however, confirm your interpretation of needs by corroborating tentative findings and by checking the performance of special student subpopulations.

Corroborate tentative findings with multiple indicators.

This may be a baseline year, but if you have used multiple indicators to look across your program, you may be more confident about what you conclude to be your strengths or weaknesses. For example, if in the first year that you collect math portfolios you find that only 12% of the students evidenced a consistent ability to explain their problem-solving strategies clearly, you will want corroborating information before overhauling this aspect of the math program. Do your classroom observations suggest that students have few opportunities to explain their work? Are students given opportunities to discuss or write about their problem-solving processes in social studies, science, or language arts? Do teacher or parent questionnaire results also suggest a weakness in this area? If several data sources tend to point in the same direction, you have identified an area of success or need.

When you organize multiple sources of data by evaluation questions, as was done in Table 5.1, it is fairly simple to find corroborating evidence for your findings from any one analysis. Here we have two sets of standardized test scores showing the same upward trend in mathematics concepts and problem solving for the past two years. The ITBS score did drop between 1989 and 1990, but, as the test norms used by the school were updated, the new norms could account for some of the drop. The comparison of Coastal Village with similar schools on the ITBS Problem Solving subtest provides further evidence of program improvement. Coastal scores are higher than Eastern and comparable to Gulf's. More students are scoring in the middle and higher ranges of the distribution at Coastal than at Gulf, however—a desirable outcome.

Look at subpopulation performance.

If you have improved and the improvement is corroborated, you're still not ready to publish your success. The same caveat applies to any initial findings of poor performance. The real purpose of evaluation is to *explain* and find solutions for program improvement, not just *describe* your school. Examine findings by subpopulation. The goal of American education is to provide equal educational opportunity for all students regardless of race, language background, or handicapping condition. Therefore you'll want to be sure that you're being equally successful with all your students.

Perhaps you have never "disaggregated" your data (looked at data by subgroups of students) before and don't know quite where to begin. Where are differences likely to occur? What should you be watching? State departments of education and large school districts generally monitor the performance of the following subpopulations:

- boys versus girls in math and in reading-writing
- limited versus redesignated versus native English proficient students
- students from different socioeconomic backgrounds, often measured by level of parent education or AFDC/free lunch participation
- students of different ethnic backgrounds: African American, Hispanic, Asian, Pacific Islander, white, and so on
- students new to the school versus those enrolled since grade 1 or 6 or 9 depending upon grade-level configurations

You may have different subgroups of interest that bear watching. Perhaps you need to look at students who have been retained one or more years (such as those participating in a prekindergarten or developmental kindergarten program). You may want to compare students who live in the neighborhood with those who are bussed to school. If you have some evidence that certain groups may be at risk for school failure, this is the time to examine their performance, however you define them.

Table 5.5 presents student survey data by subgroup, boys versus girls, for the statement, "I usually understand how to do my math assignments." We see that a larger percentage of boys affirm this statement as they move through middle school while the percentage of girls saying that they understand their assignments plummets drastically from grade 6 to 8. This raises an issue: Despite overall improvements in mathematics performance, are all students benefiting from the math program?

Your analysis of subpopulation needs should follow the same procedures as your school-level needs assessment: Look at trends over time; corroborate findings with multiple measures. In this way, you are "controlling" for random fluctuations in student population, student mobility, and less-than-perfect measures.

Sample Worksheet 5.1 summarizes strategies for answering the "how are we doing" question (needs assessment) and provides examples for answering program improvement questions as well.

TABLE 5.5 Sample Data for Answering Formative Evaluation Questions

Question: Are we implementing the math program as planned?
Teacher Interview Summaries (20 teachers)

What new strategies used?	*What problems are we having?*
Cooperative learning; n = 20	Need more planning time; n = 18
Student math projects; n = 14	No time for writing essays; n = 14
Math essays; n = 2	Kids don't know math facts; n = 7

Student Survey Summary (Grade 6 = 310; Grade 7 = 331; Grade 8 = 312)
I usually understand how to do my math assignments and homework.

Grade	*Boys*	*Girls*
6	75%	77%
7	78%	56%
8	79%	43%

Grade-8 Mathematics Portfolio Summaries (random sample of 50; 10 per classroom)

Class	*Papers*	*Essay*	*Problems*	*Mean Rating (1 - 6)*	*ITBS Concepts Mean SS*
1	40	2%	10%	2.3	210
2	17	30%	45%	4.7	245
3	10	20%	50%	4.2	234
4	4	0	1%	1.2	195
5	12	3%	10%	2.1	200
Average	16.60	11.00	23.20	3.10	216.80

Percentage of Time Spent in Cooperative Learning Groups by Grade Level Over Last 3 Years

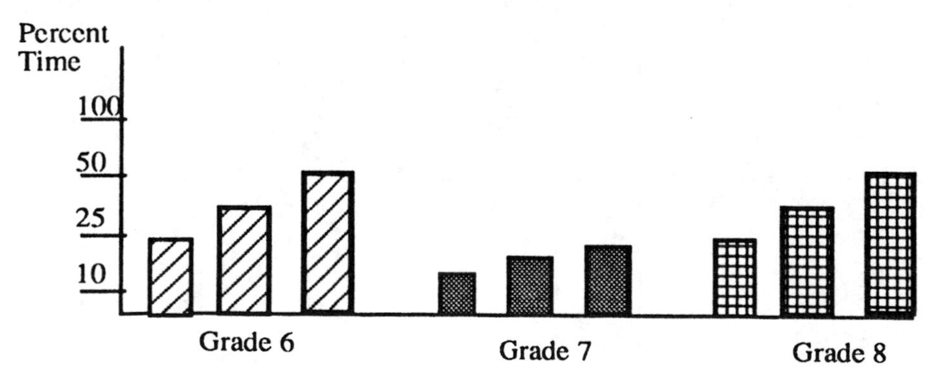

Sample Worksheet 5.1
Data Analysis for Specific Evaluation Questions

Question: In what areas are we in need of improvement?

Instrument	*Score Used*	*Analysis*
CTBS	Percentiles	Table showing percentage of students scoring in each quartile range: 0-24; 25-49; 50-74; 75-99
	Percentile	School-level percentile rank equivalent to the mean school standard score
	Derived score	Bar graph showing mean standard scores for reading, math, and language for grades 3, 4, 5, 6, (separate graphs for each grade level)
	Derived score	Line graph for reading showing mean score for last 3 years; graphs for math and language
State assessment	Percentile	Table showing percentage of students scoring in each quartile range
	Percentile	School rank in state
	Derived score	Mean scores in reading for LEP, English, FEP students; for math; for language
	Derived score	Line graph showing mean reading score for past 3 years, mean math, mean language
Competency	Percentage	Bar graph showing passing percentage for reading, writing, math Bar graph showing passing percentage age for special program students
Parent survey	Average percentage positive on program related questions	Bar graph comparing percentage agreeing with positive statements about reading, math, language

Question: How well are we implementing a process-based approach to writing?

Instrument	*Score Used*	*Analysis*
Observations	Tally of techniques observed	Table listing desirable writing strategies observed and frequency of each
Teachers	None	List of successes and obstacles reported

Question: Is student writing improving?

Instrument	*Score Used*	*Analysis*
Portfolios	Essay rating	Bar graph showing percentage of students at each grade level rated "4" or above
Student survey	Percentage saying "agree" or "strongly agree" on questions 2, 6	Bar graph showing average percentage reporting writing is improving by grade level
Teachers	None	List of specific ways teachers report writing improved; teacher estimate of percentage of students still writing well below expectations

Question: Do students feel positive about the writing program?

Instrument	*Score Used*	*Analysis*
Student survey	Percentage saying "agree" on questions 9, 11	Bar graph comparing average percentage of students with positive responses on questions 9 and 11 with average percentage of parents reporting students are positive on parent questions 5 and 9
Parent survey	Percentage saying "agree" on questions 5, 8	

Answering Formative Evaluation Questions

In analyzing data to identify school strengths and weaknesses, you look across a range of programs and develop a wide perspective; when you ask, "How can we improve?" in formative evaluation, however, you want an in-depth view of specific programs. This view is concerned with "how" and "why." You want to know more than what your performance profile is; you are concerned about finding explanations for this performance and solutions, if necessary. Involve others in this search for explanations and maintain an ongoing dialogue about the relationship between school processes and outcomes.

Check to see that you have a "program" and that it is being implemented.

One of the most common mistakes we make in looking at our school programs is to assume that, just because we call something a program, it actually exists. Your district has switched to "whole language" teaching in grades K-6, has adopted materials, and all teachers have been to two whole language in-services. Your district mentor teacher has presented a workshop on integrating reading and writing, and all administrators have been shown how to observe a whole language classroom. Suppose your evaluation questions focus on the effectiveness of this new approach. If you are interested in improving this new program, first, be sure it exists. Have teachers renamed their actions but continued with the same practices, teaching literature as they would a basal? Are there inconsistencies in implementation by grade level? What problems are you having in implementing the program? Do you have enough materials? Do you all understand it in the same or a similar way? Do you feel comfortable with new strategies needed to make it work? The answers to these questions can be found, in part, by looking at data in some of the ways suggested below:

- Look at observation and interview data. Listen to steering committee experiences. List the activities being implemented. Note problems encountered or successes attained.
- Look at student, teacher, and parent survey data. Look for agreement as to program descriptions, activities. Look for reports of desired program outcomes such as increased writing, better attitude toward mathematics, and more willingness to set aside time to study.

Program implementation data are included with the data summaries shown in Table 5.5. The teacher interview information shows an uneven use of new strategies, with cooperative learning being most widely used and writing about mathematics least implemented. Data from the student survey and a breakdown of the number of math essays in the grade-8 portfolios corroborate our supposition that teachers aren't having students write about mathematics. If this is a central component of our program, we have some evidence that it hasn't been implemented as planned. The data also suggest that teachers want more in-service in this area and are not yet comfortable with this part of the program.

Look for relationships among school context, process, and outcomes.

During the process of summarizing, you will begin to notice similar patterns in different data sources. As you calculate absence patterns by grade level, sex, and educational placement, you may note that you find more absences among students in basic courses in grades 11 to 12. These relationships may help you pinpoint areas in need of improvement or provide explanations for your outcomes. Some of the most common relationships found in studies of schools include

- socioeconomic status, length of time in school, language proficiency, and standardized test scores
- attendance and grade point average
- enrollment in academic courses and SAT, ACT, or achievement test scores
- parent involvement rates, knowledge about school programs, and school achievement
- student attitudes toward school, attendance, grades, and post-school educational plans

In our previous example from Table 5.5, we find a possible relationship between program processes and outcomes. The two classes with the most writing assignments had the highest math concepts scores and portfolio ratings. Although this could be attributable to many factors, class composition and teacher style among them, it is a relationship that we may want to know more about and monitor in the coming year.

Look for relationships between the theory underlying your action plans and predicted outcomes.

Many of the changes now taking place in our schools are those based on theories of how students learn, how teachers improve professionally, and how curriculum should be organized to produce more meaningful instruction. These theories suggest relationships between changes we are making and certain outcomes we can expect as a result. For example, when you adopt a process-based approach to writing, you expect to find a greater quantity of writing and more students feeling that everyone can learn to write, not just the talented few. Use the predictions based on the theory behind the writing process to identify relationships between practice and outcomes at your school. Having asked students on a questionnaire how much writing they have done in the past few weeks and if they feel that "anyone can learn to write," you then might look at their answers in relation to average scores on student writing samples or teacher reports about the quality of student writing. The presence of a relationship among these variables suggests that your theory is supported.

If you find no relationship, you might ask whether you have interpreted the theory correctly (is sheer quantity of writing related to improvement or does the quality of writing instruction and/or type of writing have a bearing) or whether it's being implemented as intended. When your results contradict expectations, you have identified a program area worth investigating.

Some theory-based relationships you might consider include

- recency of teacher in-service activities and implementation of new techniques,
- opportunities for teachers to try new techniques in a "safe" environment with peer support and inclination to implement an innovative strategy,
- heterogeneous student grouping for academic activities and positive attitudes toward the subject,
- use of calculators in mathematics and improved retention of number facts, and
- integration of subjects such as reading, math, writing, social studies, and science for young children and improved reading comprehension and school motivation.

In our earlier discussion of Table 5.5, we have noticed a possible relationship between the amount of writing and math test performance or portfolio rating. One reason this relationship stood out was that the theory underlying our program implementation activities suggests that, when students have an opportunity to make their own meanings of numerical relationships, they have a better understanding of mathematics. Writing about math is certainly one way to engage students in thinking about numbers and how they "work." Thus the relationship that piqued our curiosity emerged from our theory of action.

Look at subgroup performance for possible explanations.

Some of the same analyses you conducted to answer the "how are we doing" questions will be useful in ferreting out possible explanations for program success or weakness. Strategies we have found useful include the following:

- Look at achievement/results by subgroups to see if differential performance is partly responsible for results. Do we do well simply because the 20% of high-performing students raise our scores?
- Look at changes in students population or mobility rates.
- Look at the trend of variables related to student performance: attendance, length of time in the same school, socioeconomic status, language. Are increases or decreases in these variables over time coincident with achievement increases or decreases?

- Look at the curriculum offered different subgroups of students. Are differences in content/skills/pacing related to the performance of subgroups?
- Look at student, parent, and teacher survey information. Does it suggest areas of weaknesses or reasons for performance?
- Graph or calculate correlations between variables related to outcomes such as the relationship between attendance and grade point average or scores, or the relationship between years in the school at time of exiting the bilingual program.
- Look at observation and interview data as well as personal anecdotes to identify success stories and things that are working well.

Use diagnostic subscales for program improvement information.

Data can be used to point out areas for improvement or to "red flag" problems. They can be used to suggest possible reasons for success or weakness. Their diagnostic potential, however, is limited by the kind of measure used. For example, although they may provide indications of relative strength and weakness, the results of standardized tests or any solely outcome-oriented performance measures will not tell you why students performed as they did (although analysis of subtest performance may suggest missing prerequisites if the underlying skills are believed to be hierarchical). Assessments, observations, and scoring guides that include process-oriented diagnostic dimensions—based, for instance, on how students learn math, science, or social studies—however, can provide important insights about why students performed as they did. Similarly, selected response questionnaire and preference measures usually won't give you hints on how to improve but including a "comments" or "suggestions" section might.

Descriptive and narrative information can help to identify why people feel as they do or to clarify program strengths or weaknesses. Subscale results also can help to pinpoint the latter.

The subscale information of interest in our middle school mathematics program example relates to the kinds of assignments in the student portfolios. We see that the percentage of papers devoted to problem solving, analysis, and explanation is low, even when the portfolios are hefty. This subscale analysis suggests that we could improve portfolio ratings (and maybe even test score performance) by increasing the number of challenging assignments in which students are asked to interact with mathematics in a creative, meaningful way.

Sample Worksheet 5.1 maps the path for conducting an in-depth analysis of your program. It provides guidelines for answering both needs assessment (how are we doing?) and formative evaluation (how can we improve?) questions. Answer these questions and you are ready for Step Six.

Suggested Readings

Entire careers are built upon analyzing data and writing statistics books, which is probably why many published sources for this topic are virtually unfathomable by most educated Americans. We've found some that are fathomable and hope you will let us know your favorites.

Fitz-Gibbon, C. T., & Morris, L. L. (1987). *How to analyze data.* Newbury Park, CA: Sage.

This is a step-by-step manual for calculating correlation coefficients, testing differences between groups, and calculating reliability. You don't need a statistics course to understand either why or how to do these procedures. Chapter 6 on the analysis of a body of data will organize the analysis procedure for even the most uninitiated.

Jaeger, R. M. (1990). *Statistics: A spectator sport* (2nd ed.). Newbury Park, CA: Sage.

If you're hiring a consultant and expect to get back sophisticated reports, complete with significance tests and correlation coefficients, not to mention a *regression analysis,* this is the volume for you. All words, no numbers, no Greek letters. It explains why statistics are used, as well as when and how to interpret them.

Morris, L. L., Fitz-Gibbon, C. T., & Lindheim, E. (1987). *How to measure performance and use tests.* Newbury Park, CA: Sage.

This is another source with multiple uses. The final chapter on using performance test data provides guidelines for answering such commonly asked questions as these: How should students be placed in programs? How do they compare with a control/comparison group? What are results like over time? Have program objectives been met? How do results relate to participant characteristics or program variations? This book is brief, conceptual, and useful for performance data.

6

Step Six
Use Findings and Continue Program Monitoring

Overview

The tasks in Step Six are few in number but complex in execution. In this step, you make public your school's success and share your action plan for addressing any weaknesses.

The central task in Step Six is to act. After gathering and summarizing data, you spent time in Step Five to reflect upon your findings with the others most involved in your school planning process. Now you will develop a plan for publicizing successes and strengthening your program where needed. In fact, Step Six is the pathway back to Step One, because what you decide to do in the coming year as a result of your evaluation provides the focus for the next year's evaluation.

Communicate Findings

A bird's eye view of the terrain.

You may draw upon a variety of methods for communicating your evaluation results. You may share your results informally through conversations with parents, teachers, or district staff or as just one agenda item at a faculty or school site advisory meeting. You may wish to submit an informal article for the PTA newsletter or tack a note on the staff bulletin board. More formal settings could include a

presentation to the Board of Education, a report for an accreditation or school review committee, or an oral report at a parent meeting.

This section describes some techniques for tailoring your reports to specific audiences. Plan to use a variety of strategies, formal, informal, oral and written, to influence your most important audiences (see Sample Worksheet 6.1).

Take your audience into account.

Neither written nor oral presentations will necessarily report all evaluation findings. Different audiences have different concerns and levels of sophistication when it comes to understanding data. Parent audiences want to know how their school "stacks up." They expect to hear of its successes but know that their school should be working to improve in some areas, even if it is doing well on the usual indicators. Our experience with parents in high-achieving schools is that they demand improvement and want specific evidence of instructional innovation despite high test scores and college placement rates. They are skeptical of reports containing only good news and are ever watchful of the whitewash. At the same time, these very concerned and involved parents will rally to improvement efforts, devoting buckets of time and money for their schools. We also have found that parents in low-achieving schools have identical concerns with a somewhat different twist: In addition to hearing about all of the weaknesses and all of the special programs designed to improve the school, parents are usually aware of special strengths—a particular teacher, an award-winning math club, a strong kindergarten program. It is important to highlight the individual and school accomplishments for the low achieving as well as the high.

Teachers want to know both how their own students are doing and whether any instructional or curricular changes they are making have a payoff. Those who see no need to change need evidence that the change has positive results. Teachers who eagerly embrace a new program or strategy seek data to validate their beliefs and convince others. The biggest difficulty in sharing findings with teachers is that data don't always provide clear-cut answers or support for one viewpoint over another; this group then can become discouraged with the evaluation process and may remain unconvinced that any information other than teacher judgment is useful.

The Board of Education, community at large, and, increasingly, the press are less directly involved but highly interested participants. These groups are less interested in the *details* of your findings but more interested in their *credibility*. These audiences are likely to raise technical issues such as "reliability," "significance," and "validity" and are likely to want explanations and recommendations supported with data. They view your successes with pride and widely publicize them; therefore they need solid substantiation of results that say real change and/or real improvement has occurred. Neither

Sample Worksheet 6.1
Communicate and Act on Findings

		Report Format		
Audiences	*Key Concern(s)*	*Formal*	*Informal*	*Date*
Teachers:			O, H	9/23
K-2	Do children like math? Do they understand "number"?			
Grade 3	Are children learning math facts as well as concepts?			
Grade 5	Do we still have the same number eligible for accelerated math at the intermediate level?			
All teachers	Are we doing it right? Are we keeping up with the other schools?			
Students:	None this time			
Parents:			O—School Advisory	10/3
K-2	Do kids like math? Are they keeping up?	P—PTA		11/7
3-5	Are kids developing "skills"? Do they have homework? Can they solve problems?	P—Parent Education Night	O—Open House	1/14 5/10
School Board:	Are the students maintaining or improving? What are you doing to improve program?	T—Prior to meeting P—Regular meeting		9/12 9/20

continued

Sample Worksheet 6.1
Continued

		Report Format		
Audiences	*Key Concern(s)*	*Formal*	*Informal*	*Date*
Community: None				
District/Other Administrators	How's it going? What should we borrow? What kind of trouble are the teachers giving you about the new math program? Are you keeping up?		O—regular principal meetings	8/21 9/12 10/3
Other: *Coastal Village Voice*	What new and interesting things in math are happening at your school.	N—formal press release		9/20

Key for entering report format:
H = Handouts: tables, sample items/performance tasks, score summaries, and so on
N = Newsletter: school, district, PTA
O = Oral, informal report: faculty meetings, district meetings
P = Presentation: formal, with invited audience, agenda, overheads, and so on
T = Technical report: formal, written report following format of research report

they nor you want to be embarrassed by random reversals in next year's results.

When you discuss areas needing improvement, a school board will most likely want to know the specifics of your action plan, with the focus on *action*. It is the group least likely to think that spending a year studying possible solutions is a reasonable first step to take in solving your school's dropout problem.

Formal, written reports.

Although you should plan to communicate your findings in a variety of forms, certainly, formal, written reports will be part of the process. Your most useful reports will be targeted to specific audiences and their concerns. Research conducted at the Center for Student Standards and Testing at UCLA on the use of information for school-based decision making pinpoints some useful guidelines for written reports targeted to site-level administrators and school boards. The guidelines summarized in Table 6.1 boil down to three rules of thumb:

- Keep your report brief and simple.
- Target your report to your audience's interests.
- Use words and pictures as well as numbers to illustrate your points.

Formal reports: School accountability report cards.

Repeatedly throughout this guide, we have referred to school accountability report cards as an impetus for evaluation as well as a vehicle for highlighting school success. Although developing the first version may require enormous time and effort, once the report card categories are identified and defined, an appropriate format worked out, and the process automated, you will discover that your evaluation efforts make annual updates easy. We have included examples of two different school report cards meeting California accountability requirements, one from an elementary school and one from a middle school (see Resource E). Note how the format and level of specificity can vary while still meeting state reporting requirements.

Formal reports: The media.

Some of your results will be reported in the newspapers or, for the less fortunate among us, on television. Your media debut most often occurs when and because the state has released test scores, not because you have called a press conference. Your local reporter will need *lots* of help understanding what scores mean, why they don't improve rapidly, and why they can fluctuate so much yet still not reflect "significant differences" in performance from one year to the next. We have found that, when we provide examples of test items, it is welcomed by the press. Most need quite a bit of education about measurement error and what a test score represents. Being able to bring to light other data bearing on school success also helps alleviate test score pressure.

TABLE 6.1 Hints for Creating Useful Reports

Both school principals and school board members say that a useful report

- is brief,
- contains narrative or explanatory information,
- presents trends over time in graphic form to support conclusions, and
- has a technical appendix for those interested in more detail.

There are some differences in report content found useful by the two groups.

- School-level administrators are most interested in the *why* and *how* of student outcomes. They seek information clarifying relationships between school policies, curriculum and instruction, and school outcomes.
- At the board level, not unexpectedly, the central concern is with the *status* of school performance and a description of progress rather than the nuts and bolts of planned improvements or reasons for performance.
- When sharing information with school boards, there is a danger in presenting information at a level of detail and complexity that is not needed.

Both audiences use and value qualitative information in decision making.

- Written reports that include summaries of carefully conducted observations, interviews, or attitude surveys will provide powerful information for program improvement.
- Teachers, principals, and others form conclusions about school effectiveness and hypotheses about how programs succeed or fail based on impressions and experiences.
- A few well-selected anecdotes also can be a powerful device for communicating the meaning of your findings.
- Explanations of school results generated during the data interpretation process form yet another source of useful information for school-level decisions.
- Qualitative data form an important part of the decision- making process; summaries of these data belong in written reports.

Informal reports: Within the school.

Although formal, written reports for outside (nonschool) audiences probably will be prepared after all data are in and interpreted, school-level constituencies will find information most useful and will be more willing to cooperate in data collection if feedback is fairly immediate. Teachers and other school staff form the closest, and perhaps most important, audience for reporting results. Most have been involved in one or more aspects of the school planning or improvement effort as well as in data collection. Reporting to teachers and staff creates an occasion to clarify and amplify proposed explanations for findings and actions for the coming year.

Remember that most people are most interested in the data that affect them personally. Parents, for example, will be very interested in preliminary results of the parent survey. Teachers will be anxious to learn about how the student portfolios fared. We have a bulletin board posted outside our office on which we post interesting feedback from teachers who are pilot testing materials so that the curriculum developers get more immediate feedback. Teachers also show great interest.

When reported promptly, even in rough form, data may help initiate some midcourse corrections. One intermediate school in the Los Angeles area found a surprising discrepancy between parent and student responses to a questionnaire sent out in January prior to developing their school plan for the next year. The question was this: "Students at this school respect others with different backgrounds." More than 90% of the parents and teachers responded that they agreed with this statement, but only 60% of the students registered the same feeling. Instead of waiting to address this issue in the next year's plan, the principal shared these preliminary results with the student council, who confirmed the student perceptions. The principal then worked with teachers to set up a special team-building cross-grade homeroom that met twice a week for the last quarter of the year and helped students to know each other better.

Informal reports: The parent-staff advisory committee.

Another important reporting forum is the regularly scheduled school advisory committee meetings—whether the bilingual, special education, gifted, school improvement, Chapter 1, or consolidated program meetings. Advisory committees generally have a long agenda and little time; reports should answer the few, focused questions of special interest to the group: How are these special populations doing? What do we plan to do to improve? How can we publicize and celebrate their successes?

Informal reports: In conjunction with other school business.

When you send your standardized test scores home to parents, you have another opportunity for sharing evaluation findings and implementing part of your school's action plan. Parents want to know how to help their children. Test score reporting provides an opportunity for your school to focus not only on individual scores but on how parents can become involved in the children's education. We have found that group meetings with parents that allow them to review their child's answer sheet and see actual items have raised parents' consciousness about testing. In 10 years of such meetings, a parent has never failed to make a public statement about how little the test reflects what the child has done in school that year. The parent forums present opportunities for sharing schoolwide patterns of test score performance and for discussing curricular changes that either account for this performance or may not be reflected in that performance. Although parents may not always be interested in attending an evening meeting to discuss new techniques used in the reading or mathematics program, they are extremely interested in their children's test scores. You can use this interest to segue to a discussion of the larger issues of their child's education.

Excerpts of your findings, from how your school stacks up compared with others to unique school successes, can be reported in your regular PTA newsletters or at school functions such as Open House. High school principals appear particularly adept at integrating "good news" evaluation findings; one of our acquaintances announced the (very positive) results of the state assessment at high school graduation! When reporting to your community, remember that many are unsophisticated consumers of data and have little knowledge of how schools operate. You should present your information in context and provide concrete examples both of the questions asked to gather the data (test items, survey questions, observation dimensions) and the action you plan to take based on the data. Even success requires action. Upon hearing "good news," parents and others ask, "What are you going to do to let others know how well we're doing?"

Develop an Action Plan

In the process of analyzing and interpreting your findings, you no doubt at least touched on their action implications. Now is the time to set your priorities.

Build upon your strengths.

During your discussions, you identified those things you were doing well as well as the areas needing more attention. Do not, as many of us are wont, focus solely upon school weaknesses. If you are improving, make public your improvements to parents, district officials, and the larger community. If you are continuing to "hold your own" despite budget cuts, increasing class size, less aide time, or increasing enrollment, recognize your success and document it. If students and teachers perceive that something is working well, for example, the peer tutoring program, but parents either know nothing about it or discount it, spend some time with your key planners discussing how you can educate your public.

But perhaps the most important consideration in reviewing school strengths and positive findings is how to build upon them in your action plan for the coming year. If you find that all English teachers have tried cooperative learning techniques in teaching writing and that most students like the group work associated with writing, think about how this technique could be used to strengthen other programs. Could your school consider using cooperative learning to improve the poorly received, heterogeneously grouped mathematics classes? Could your English teachers serve as "coaches" for the mathematics teachers who wish to try cooperative learning? Does your school have a really outstanding program in the arts, in interdisciplinary education, bilingual education, or multicultural education? Perhaps you should apply for special funding in one of these areas using the results of your evaluation to support your claims of program effectiveness.

Have you found improvement in many areas? Perhaps this is the year to consider applying for a state or national distinguished school award or to join a network of schools dedicated to sharing program ideas in mathematics, technology, parent eduction, or other special programs. All schools have successes to share and improvement to publicize. Be sure to incorporate these successes into your plans for the next year.

Address weaknesses.

"Weakness" is a term with many meanings. To a high-achieving school with much community support, weakness is relative. In such idyllic circumstances, you could ask the question, "How do we keep on doing as well as we have in the past?" rather than the question, "How can we do better?" The action plan for such a school will use trends spotted in the evaluation data to anticipate potential future problems and attempt to solve them before they actually become problems. For example, a high-achieving school may have adopted a whole language reading-writing program but continue to test students with multiple choice tests. The evaluation findings may show that reading test scores remain high but language scores have dropped a bit. When whole language programs are implemented, student performance on discrete skills tests often falls, even though there are other program benefits. In this situation, the school could dedicate one section of its action plan to educating parents and the press about the mismatch between the standardized testing program and the new whole language program. It could also decide to use and report to the public results of more holistic assessments such as writing samples or reading-writing portfolios. A third action could be to teach children how to answer multiple choice tests and how the strategy is different than those used in reading and understanding a large chunk of prose.

Some schools find that they are deluged with weaknesses from low scores to poor attendance to high student mobility to low parent involvement to a lack of bilingual instructors and little money for new supplies or in-service. The best strategy in this situation is this: Focus on doing a few things well. Here is where your evaluation findings will be really helpful. As you analyzed your data, you looked for relationships among school context factors or program strategies and outcomes. Identify the most powerful relationships you found. Will monitoring attendance improve the parents' perceptions of the school and academic achievement as well as garner community support? Will reorganizing the primary grade program and instituting developmental, ungraded education address the readiness and retention problems? Will adding counselors improve attendance and enrollment in academic courses and prevent dropouts?

Continue Program Monitoring

Document your plan.

An action plan is simply your goals for the coming year and the strategies you will employ to meet those goals. The plan may be informal or it may already be a required component of a mandated school planning process, a formal plan that you file at the district each year. If you have special funding, your action plan is actually part of your school plan, perhaps Chapter 1 or Title VII goals.

Your action plan also may be built into the staff evaluation process. You and the staff could incorporate at least one strategy to address a school need. Whether your action plan is a separate document, part of the school site plan, notations in the school calendar, or a set of goals to incorporate into the staff evaluation process, it is a commitment both to ongoing school improvement and to ongoing monitoring of your school's progress. Once you have devoted the time and resources to conduct a careful evaluation of school needs or of a particular program, you have set in motion a self-sustaining process for tracking your success.

This brings us right back to Step One in the evaluation process, focusing your evaluation. The *results* of your first evaluation provide the *focus* for the second, and so the cycle is repeated. As with the example cited earlier in the development of a school report card, once the initial time has been spent exploring issues of concern to school constituencies, training an advisory group to think in terms of school context, processes, and outcomes, and gathering or developing a set of locally valid, reliable, and credible tracking strategies, the process becomes automated.

We have completed the last step of sensible school-based evaluation. Although we have seen that acting on your findings and continuing to monitor your programs lead us right back to Step One, you will be relieved to know that, for those not wanting to follow the logical sequence of events, which is to begin reading Step One again, we offer an exit to this guide that not only gets you out of the loop but moves you up to another view of tracking your success.

Suggested Readings

As reporting your findings will most likely be one of your actions, we highlight several sources for reporting information to various audiences.

Bain, J. G., & Herman, J. L. (1989). *Improving opportunities for underachieving minority students: A planning guide for community action.* Los Angeles: CRESST.
If your evaluation results point to improving community involvement, this handbook provides a step-by-step approach for accomplishing your plan. Full of worksheets and procedures, you'll find templates and ideas for many kinds of action plans.

Frechtling, J. A., & Myerberg, N. J. (1983). *Reporting test scores to different audiences* (ERIC/TM Report 85). Princeton, NJ: ERIC Clearinghouse on Tests, Measurement and Evaluation.
These well-known evaluators from Montgomery County, Maryland, have reviewed the testing reports from major school districts and developed guidelines for improving test reporting practices. This guide will help you present your successes clearly and keep you from making the most common mistakes in reporting test scores.

Herman, J. L. (1989). *Political and practical issues in improving school boards' use of evaluation data.* Los Angeles: CRESST.
This paper summarizes field interviews with school board members. Unlike Freud, Herman did find an answer to her question, "What do school board members want?" The answer could save your career.

Morris, L. L., Fitz-Gibbon, C. T., & Freeman, M. E. (1987). *How to communicate evaluation findings.* Newbury Park, CA: Sage.
A whole book on reporting and it's about time! We like the parts dedicated to dealing with difficult audiences and the press (are they different?).

Reprise and Revelation

Evaluation Is Much Faster the Second Time Around

You have just been through a six-step evaluation process adapted especially for school people to help them look at their own schools. Although school-based evaluation may appear intimidating, remember, you largely are just making explicit many of the processes you currently go through implicitly. You are building in some extra time and productively involving constituencies as you address routine school tasks, such as revising your school improvement or Chapter 1 school plan, preparing accountability reports for the district or state, or getting ready for routine district and state program reviews. Sensible school-based evaluation requires that you approach these tasks with thoughtful questioning about what you plan to do and how you will know you have accomplished your plans. Sensible evaluation involves advance planning about the various kinds of information, most of which is already available at your school, that you will routinely gather throughout the course of a year to inform your school-level planning and decision making.

The first time through, this process takes time: time for meetings to clarify school goals and identify concerns, time to find or develop progress tracking strategies, time to organize and review results, and time to bring people aboard in the decision-making process. Once you have identified appropriate instruments, specified scoring strategies and reports, trained teachers and others in scoring strategies, figured out analysis strategies, and created report formats, the process becomes "built in."

Watch how much easier and faster school-based evaluation becomes the second time around.

Step One. Focus the evaluation.

This time, your evaluation questions will emerge naturally from your analyses and interpretations of your first year's effort. If, during the first year, you conducted a needs assessment to profile your school strengths and weaknesses, the areas that you determined needed attention and the plans you identified for addressing them would be the focus of the second-year evaluation. For example, you may have found that you didn't meet all the standards you set in areas such as dropout rate, mathematics achievement, parent satisfaction with the mathematics program, and student perceptions of intergroup toleration and cooperation. On that basis, you formulated some improvement plans. These improvement plans subsequently could provide a focus for a year-two *formative* evaluation effort in which you ask the question, "How effective are the planned improvements?" If you are in the enviable position of having met all your standards, you may wish to look at the performance of potentially at-risk subgroups of students to identify their special needs or to look at state mandates regarding the implementation of a new assessment program or a new mathematics program to provide a focus for school planning and evaluation. Regardless of the specific circumstances in your school, your year-two evaluation questions will emerge naturally as you interpret year-one findings and develop an action plan. Thus the time you spent during the first year's evaluation in bringing together important constituencies and initiating discussions about possible evaluation questions will not be necessary this second time around. These tasks will have been completed during the development of your action plan.

Step Two. Identify tracking strategies.

The measures you adapted, selected, or developed during year one can be used in the second year. You may have to change a few questions on the parent survey or tighten up the scoring rubrics for the science demonstrations, but your year-one measures can remain essentially intact for year two. If you should decide to look at completely different areas, ask yourself if the "student attitudes toward reading" survey can be adapted to measuring your new focus, such as attitudes toward science. Or can your history portfolios serve as a model for developing a mathematics portfolio? Can the standardized test you used to look at school needs during year one serve a more diagnostic function in year two if you order different kinds of scores such as item analyses or reports of average grade-level performance by objectives? If your school records were less than useful during year one, can you change the record keeping system to make them useful now?

Step Three. Manage instrument development and data collection.

Your data collection schedule, if successful, can serve as a model for year two. Your experience will help you adjust dates if some of your time lines were too short. Remember, instrument development will not take up quite so much time this year, as you most likely will be adapting year-one measures whenever possible. You also may feel that conducting a written parent survey is not necessary every year. You could consider sampling over a two- or three-year cycle and getting input from your school advisory committee and PTA during the intervening years.

You now have trained data collectors, perhaps even parent volunteers, and teachers proficient at scoring some types of performance assessments. You will save time (and money) if you can use some of these people during the second year. We have found that, once we have a data collection schedule that accommodates school holidays, Open House, and parent conference days, scheduling for subsequent years will remain the same with only the minor adjustment of changing exact calendar dates. Your data collection plan simply can be part of the school master calendar.

Step Four. Scoring and summarizing data.

You made your major scoring decisions and specified score reports the first year. You also provided training for essay ratings, portfolios, and the like. As long as these trained staff are still at your school, you need only plan a refresher prior to scoring. You also can order or use many of the same score reports. Scoring becomes a more automated process. With archival data, scoring can be simplified if you have computerized records, a topic to which we return later. In any case, the time spent in scoring decisions is significantly reduced if you use the same or similar measures a second time.

Step Five. Analyze information and interpret findings.

Use the data presentation techniques that worked best with your advisory committee as templates for presenting year-two data. Again, having computer templates will speed up the process, but, even in their absence, the process of thinking through your data analyses the second and subsequent times around will be much faster and easier. You no longer have to decide *how* to organize information and try out different display strategies until you find the most useful ones.

One place you will not want to stint on time, however, will be the actual process of reviewing your findings with involved constituencies. The heart of the evaluation process is interpretation and judgment. What happened? Was it good or bad? Why did it occur? How do we do better? These issues, though the same every year, have no fast answers and are always more clearly understood from multiple perspectives. "Protecting" teachers from the sometimes contentious discussion of school results has the unfortunate side effect of losing an important perspective in school improvement. Although not everyone is elated at the prospect of looking at tables and graphs or model portfolios at a 3:15 p.m. faculty meeting, you just never know what kinds of observations and explanations about school performance will be uttered from the back row. "Outlier" interpretations and viewpoints may stimulate unconventional solutions to heretofore intractable problems.

Although the amount of time needed to look at findings may not be less the second time around, people will be more comfortable using data and will need less time to understand tables and graphs. You may find some who look forward to the process because, for the first time, they see "hard evidence" to back up what they know to be occurring in the classroom. This validation of teacher judgment holds a central position in sensible school-based evaluation.

Step Six. Use findings and continue program monitoring.

The reporting formats that worked well during year one become templates for year two. These formats go beyond accountability report cards and can include presentations at parent meetings or board presentations. Most likely, your school board is too busy (hopefully not with budget cuts) to hear from you every year, which cuts down the time needed to prepare a formal written technical evaluation report. On the other hand, parents may come to expect and look forward to an annual "testing" or "school evaluation" report from which they can get more information about their children's testing program, school expectations and standards, and how your particular curriculum and instructional strategies are meeting their children's needs. We have found that we created a monster by staging annual parent testing meetings, but, when we fed the monster information about the tests and the curriculum, it was a beast that toiled for and supported us. (And updating the overheads was pretty simple the second time around.)

Similarly, the process of monitoring your action plan is more easily incorporated into your daily activities the second time around. Because you and your staff know the year's focus and have generated the questions you want answered, nearly everyone has antenna raised to detect information related to your school's plan. And, being thinking human beings, for every piece of information, someone has an explanation or idea that can be incorporated into the plan for next year. If your action plan is stimulated by a mandate to develop a school accountability report card each year, program monitoring in the report card areas becomes something all staff attend to in some fashion (even if it's just to grumble about it). As for developing your action plan (i.e., your school goals) for the following year, you will probably find ideas and the focus emerging from your discussion of findings during Step Five, which brings us back to Step One and focusing your subsequent evaluation. Pretty painless, wasn't it?

It's Not Too Late to Automate

At this point in our discussion of the evaluation process, we're beginning to feel like the introductory statistics professor who insists you calculate correlation coefficients by hand so you will understand the process, because you really don't have to conduct your evaluation "by hand." If you have noticed something familiar in our reprise, you will have observed that the words *automate* and *template* pepper the text. These two words bring to mind our friend the computer. Should you have access to a personal computer, it is simple to automate the more tedious and labor-intensive aspects of the evaluation process.

What to automate. Prior to purchasing equipment or software or to dedicating any part of a computer system to evaluation functions, you should specify what you need to automate. What tasks you need performed will determine the equipment and software required. The following tasks are naturals for automation.

Focus the evaluation:

- data base with the names and addresses of school advisory groups for producing mailing labels (if your school is completely automated, use electronic mail for meeting notifications and reminders)
- word processing files containing meeting minutes and brainstorming suggestions for evaluation focus

Identify tracking strategies:

- text data base with items for questionnaires, observations, interviews, curriculum-related tests, performance tests for creating new forms of instruments
- if you have no text data base (such as Notebook III), use your word processing program and revise measures with cut-and-paste procedures

Plan data collection:

- automate your calendar and create a "tickler" file to remind you of tasks to be done each day/week
- purchase project-management software

Score and summarize data:

- data base for scores or responses that will create list reports and summaries and calculate means
- graphing program to graph results

Analyze and interpret data:

- data base that "talks to" a spreadsheet or simple statistical package and allows you to calculate statistics using performance test ratings, test scores, or proportions of response to questionnaire items
- student data base and analysis/reporting templates to track performance and other indicators over time

Act on findings and monitor your action plan:

- templates for your school plan based on state or program (Chapter 1, Title VII, and so on) requirements
- template for your school accountability report card
- templates for your PTA newsletter or press releases
- templates for parent presentation overheads
- templates for district school board reports
- templates for teacher evaluations observation notes (useful for personnel and program evaluation)

Hardware considerations. You will, of course, need a computer and some software that allows you to store information, sort it in several ways, create summary reports of that information, and maybe even graph it. This means that you will need a computer with at least 20 MB of hard disk storage to hold the newer user-friendly programs that take up so much space, such as Windows or the Mac graphics-based programs, as well as your data. If you have a large school (say 1,000 students or more), you will appreciate having speedy disk access. As for computer peripherals, you will need a printer and a monitor. If your school has a well-heeled patron, ask for a laser printer (wonderful for producing accountability report cards), a page display monitor, a scanner for reading text into the computer, and a data scanner. Plan to get expert advice on what to buy and how to set up necessary programs and programming routines.

You should know that Scan-tron has a test analysis package that you can install on a microcomputer that you hook up to a Scan-tron scoring machine. The package allows you to create score reports for any kind of measure that has selected responses, including questionnaires and tests that allow more than one correct answer. You may wish to investigate this option if your school is a large one and has to score and report minimum proficiency tests on a routine basis. The software is especially useful for analyzing survey data because it prints out the number and percentage of people responding to each answer choice on each survey question as well as item means. Calculating this information by hand very quickly becomes extremely tedious.

Software possibilities. You have several software options for automating evaluation functions. You could purchase a school-based evaluation system similar to the one devised for an elementary school by Bill Cooley at LRDC in Pittsburgh, Pennsylvania (Bank & Williams, 1985), described in the bibliography for this chapter. You could purchase a software system devised specifically for schools that has scheduling, attendance, and testing modules that summarize data useful for evaluation. Another option is to use your existing software. At a minimum, you will need the following capabilities:

- Word processing: templates for data display and tables; templates for school report cards; templates for reports and newsletter articles; "item bank" of questionnaires, observations, and performance tasks and rubrics
- Spreadsheet: for calculating averages, standard deviations, percentages, and other summary statistics and for creating simple data displays with bar or line graphs
- Data base (sometimes incorporated into the spreadsheet or word processing program): for storing attendance data, test

scores, and any codable/quantifiable information that you may want to sort in different ways and for creating different kinds of reports

Many of us already have "integrated" programs that perform two or more of the above functions. Microsoft Works, Appleworks, Q&A, Excel, or Word Perfect are examples. We would caution you against using full-tilt relational, stand-alone, data base systems that require a programmer to enter data and develop reports or any program that you are unable to use after initial training. If you are shopping for data management software, tear out the questions listed below and refer to them surreptitiously as you query the salespeople:

- "What kind of training do I need to use this software?"
- "How many cases [individual student records] will it handle?"
- "How long will it take to sort 1,000 records? 2,000? [or number of your choice?]"
- "How long will it take to run lists or labels for 1,000 [or number of your choice] students?"
- "Show me some reports produced by your system that are similar to these [produce your score reports and data summaries from year one—that's why we had you go through the process first]. Can your system do this? If so, what do I need to do to produce this report?"
- "What kind of free technical support is available?"
- "How compatible are files from this software with [name your word processing and spreadsheet programs]?"

If you have software capable of calculating means, medians, modes, percentages, and creating bar and line graphs, you have the basic tools for analyzing evaluation data. There may be times you need to call in an expert for more sophisticated statistical analysis procedures (or you wish to do them yourself, perhaps as a graduate school assignment). For these occasions, you will need to have at least passing knowledge of what kinds of files your data management program produces (you will need an ASCII file for most applications) and what kinds of files the statistical software package will import.

As you consider automating all or part of the evaluation process, the natural question arises: "When do I need to bring in help?" Here is the second revelation of this chapter: You may need to call in a consultant.

Getting by With a Little Help From Your Friends

It could be that you have no intention of conducting an evaluation on your own. You are sitting on big bucks and all you want to do is to hire someone to get the job done. Or it could be that, after reading this guide, you have identified areas where you feel overwhelmed or where bringing in an expert would save you time or money. Or you perhaps have access to district, county, or state evaluation consultants who can't shepherd you through the entire process but who could, if used at key times, make the process move more smoothly.

You should consider bringing in a consultant, at least the first time around to work with you every step of the way or just at strategic points (depending on your resources). For either strategy, we recommend you find someone who understands schools, preferably *your* kind of school, and who has expertise in the areas where you feel least confident.

- Bring in someone who is technically experienced and who understands schools. This does not mean a graduate student in statistics or a teacher working on an advanced degree in administration. Look for someone with expertise in evaluation and assessment as well as experienced in schools (with grade levels similar to those in your school).
- Ask for a work sample; look at the writing and the presentation. Can you understand what is being written? Do the conclusions follow both from the evidence and from what you know about schools? Is the text reader friendly? Are the methods carefully described? Are results supported by data rather than intuition?
- Interview the candidates and look to see if they understand what your school is attempting to do and trying to accomplish. Look for an ability to relate to teachers and others on staff. Be sure that the candidate listens to your concerns and is willing to come up with new or at least adapt his or her strategies to your school. Beware of the consultant who uses the same design or the same techniques for every situation.
- Review the consultant's resume for experience in doing the kinds of things that will be most difficult for your staff (e.g., considering and devising a variety of assessment instruments, figuring out scoring schemes, running reliability analyses, specifying and conducting appropriate analyses).

Whether you have a consultant work with you every step of the way or use one at key points, the following are the most crucial areas and where you'll want to spend your time and money.

Focusing. If this is your first attempt at school-level planning and evaluation, and you are facing a somewhat hostile staff, you may wish to bring in a neutral, friendly consultant to set up an open and accepting environment for focusing activities. The expert can help in getting people to clarify their evaluation concerns, without them thinking you're looking for particular answers, and can help you select the kinds of questions that will be most informative for your particular situation.

Tracking strategies. At this stage, you'll want a consultant who already is familiar with a wide range of published measures, with measures and strategies being used successfully in schools like yours, and with the entire instrument development process. Especially important will be selecting someone with actual experience using the kinds of measures you will be using.

If you are doing any kind of performance assessment, you probably need a consultant, if only to train your "lead" teachers, for designing or adapting performance tasks, for developing scoring rubrics with staff, for training scorers, and for assuring that credible levels of scoring reliability are met.

Instrument development and data collection. As discussed in the previous step, instrument development can be a quagmire for the novice. As you wish your results to be credible and defensible, you should seriously consider getting help, or at least expert review, if you plan to develop your own questionnaires, observation scales, interview questions, or curriculum-based tests and performance assessments. Data collection, on the other hand, is labor intensive. You will probably not want to spend your "expert" consultant dollars on a person to copy data from archives, to walk into classrooms and administer standardized tests, or to make follow-up phone calls to parents who haven't returned their questionnaires. You may want to have an expert assist with classroom observations or staff interviews to provide another, more neutral, perspective on your findings.

Scoring and summarizing. For published tests, this process is done by the test-scoring service. For performance tests, bringing in an expert, at least for the first time, can provide a wonderful staff development opportunity. Developing scoring criteria, conducting rating sessions, and establishing rater reliability require experience and expertise worth the expenditure. On the other hand, you probably don't need any special advice at all to score and summarize questionnaire data, unless it's to set up automated computer programs. If you have videotapes of classrooms, extensive scripts of classroom observations, or other kinds of narrative data, you may want help in setting up scoring categories and creating a procedure for rater reliability.

Analyze and interpret findings. As with instrument development, here is an area worth some expenditure. The expert can determine what kinds of statistics should be used to summarize data, create score reports, and synthesize data from several sources. The expert can help your advisory committee look at the tables, graphs, model portfolios, and other information needed to answer your evaluation questions and can demystify the data interpretation process. You will find you get your money's worth if you create a teaching relationship between your consultant and the school; get your expert to train you in how to analyze and interpret findings.

Act on findings, continue to monitor your program.

It's not likely that anyone but school staff can do this job. You may wish to use an expert, however, to write any formal, technical evaluation reports that will be subject to public, perhaps hostile, scrutiny and that will have to stand up under tough questioning. You might have an expert share the podium at a parent education evening or present findings to staff (we've found that high school principals don't mind having a little help from their friends once in a while). An outside consultant could even set up your accountability report card template. Beyond these areas, communicating findings and acting upon them remains the province of the school.

Tracking Your Success: The Road to Success

As you have accompanied us through the steps in tracking your success, we hope you have been able to discover for your own particular school the benefits of evaluation activities. We view evaluation as a decision-making process, something we all do intuitively, though not always systematically. Sensible school-based evaluation simply systematizes a very human activity: Ask a question, get information, make a judgment/decision. We hope, too, that we have communicated the importance of focusing on your success or on strategies of attaining success through program improvement rather than on focusing on "remediation" and "explanation."

We firmly believe that school improvement is built upon the successes we have already attained or the standards for success we hold. In tracking, or hunting down, these successes, we engage in a process that helps us identify important relationships among school contexts, processes, and outcomes. When we do identify these relationships and can replicate them, we have given ourselves powerful tools for school improvement. When we find out, for example, that, when teachers allow students to collaborate on assignments in heterogeneously grouped mathematics classrooms, both the academic performance and the self-concept of students of all abilities improve, we have powerful evidence of school success as well as a pathway for reaching our success in other programs.

We hope that you will find reading this guide as useful as we have in writing it for clarifying our thoughts about evaluation, especially as conducted by school staff in a local setting to address immediate needs. We also hope that we leave you better informed consumers of evaluation results and better able to hire the kind of expertise that will help you make your school the success you know it can be. And, because we live in California, where the bumper sticker mentality still prevails, our parting words are these: Keep on Tracking!

Suggested Readings

We have three major suggestions here: (a) As a reprise of the evaluation process, read the *Evaluator's Handbook* referred to in Step Three or any of the books mentioned in the Introduction. (b) If you wish to automate, we have a few suggestions below, but the advice is still, know as much as you can about what you want prior to undertaking the task. (c) If you find yourself in the enviable position of being able to hire help, again, the *Handbook* provides a good overview. By this stage, you're well steeped in evaluation lore and it's time to act. We have a few suggestions, however, for the armchair evaluator:

Alkin, M. C. (1990). *Debates on evaluation.* Newbury Park, CA: Sage.
For those who haven't outgrown the *Playboy*-interview format, this book has interviews with prominent evaluators throughout the nation on such topics as evaluation theory, use, and ethics. As what these evaluators think eventually gets implemented in evaluation guidelines for schools, we have an interesting peek at the future as well as at current dilemmas.

Bank, A., & Williams, R. C. (Eds.). (1985). *Information systems and school improvement.* New York: Teachers' College Press.
Computomania peaked about this time, so we have a still-current view of how to use computers for school improvement. Sirotnik and Burstein's chapter, "Making Sense Out of Comprehensive School-Based Information Systems," provides an in-depth view of how one high school consolidated information needs. You'll also find the chapters by Bill Cooley and Robert Blum on automating the elementary school and creating a school profile germane.

Resource A: Sample Parent Survey

Name: ______________________ F[ ] M[ ] Date: ______ Interviewer: ____________________
Phone: ( ) __________ Relationship to student (mother, father, guardian, etc.): ______
Student's Name: ______________________ F[ ] M[ ] School/Teacher: ________/__________
Student's Grade Level: _____ Language of Interview: Spanish English Other: ________

1. What do you know about the Model Technology Program at your school? (Write exact quote)

2. Please answer the following questions by indicating the number that corresponds to your response.

	Almost Never	Rarely	Some-times	Often	Almost Always	Not Sure/ Don't Know
a. My child enjoys going to school.	1	2	3	4	5	6
b. My child talks to me about what s/he does in school.	1	2	3	4	5	6
c. My child likes to do schoolwork on computers.	1	2	3	4	5	6
d. My child likes to do schoolwork with video equipment.	1	2	3	4	5	6
e. My child talks to me about his/her schoolwork with computers and other technology.	1	2	3	4	5	6
f. I am satisfied with how much my child learns in school.	1	2	3	4	5	6

3. In which *three* academic subjects would you like to see your child improve the most? PROBE

a. ____ English language skills
b. ____ Spanish language skills
c. ____ Math
d. ____ Social Studies
e. ____ Science
f. ____ Spelling
g. ____ Reading
h. ____ Speaking
i. ____ other ________
j. ____ other ________
k. ____ other ________

4. How satisfied are you with your child's progress in the following areas:

	Not at All	Very Little	Some	A Lot	A Great Deal	NA/ Don't Know
Reading	1	2	3	4	5	6
Math	1	2	3	4	5	6
Writing	1	2	3	4	5	6

Science	1	2	3	4	5	6
Social Studies	1	2	3	4	5	6
Peer Relationships	1	2	3	4	5	6
Self-Confidence	1	2	3	4	5	6
Cultural Sensitivity	1	2	3	4	5	6
Motivation for Learning	1	2	3	4	5	6

The following questions are intended to gather information about parents as a group. Remember, answers to the next questions as well as to all of the questions you have answered will be kept strictly confidential.

5. How long have you lived in this community? _______ years

6. What language(s) is (are) used primarily in your home?

[ ]	[ ]	[ ]	[ ]
Mostly English	Mostly Spanish	About the same amounts of English and Spanish	Other language(s) Please Specify: ____________

7. What is the highest grade level in school that you have completed? ________________

   Where did you go to school? ____

8. What is your marital status?
   [ ] Married [ ] Divorced [ ] Widowed [ ] Separated [ ] Single

9. What is the employment status of the adults in your household?
   (Count adult #1 as respondent)

Adult #1:	Employed P-T [ ]	F-T [ ]	Unemployed [ ]	In school P-T [ ]	F-T [ ]
Adult #2:	Employed P-T [ ]	F-T [ ]	Unemployed [ ]	In school P-T [ ]	F-T [ ]
Adult #3:	Employed P-T [ ]	F-T [ ]	Unemployed [ ]	In school P-T [ ]	F-T [ ]
Adult #4:	Employed P-T [ ]	F-T [ ]	Unemployed [ ]	In school P-T [ ]	F-T [ ]

10. Are there any additional comments or suggestions that you would like to make at this time?

THANK YOU!

Resource B: Sample Teacher Survey

Please indicate your responses by checking, circling, or filling in the blanks.

1. Sex: [ ]M [ ]F

2. Ethnicity [ ] Caucasian [ ] Latino [ ] Native American
   [ ] Black [ ] Asian [ ] Other__________

3. How many years *including this one* have you participated in the project? ____________

Academic/Professional Background

4. What is the highest degree you have received?
   [ ] Bachelor's + teaching credential
   [ ] Bachelor's + units beyond credential
   [ ] Master's
   [ ] Master's + units beyond
   [ ] Doctorate
   [ ] Other (specify) ________________

5. Please indicate which teaching credentials you have and specify the content area of specialization. (Check ALL that apply.)
   [ ] General Elementary
   [ ] General Secondary
   [ ] Special Emergency
   [ ] Multiple Subject
   [ ] Single Subjects
   [ ] Bilingual
   [ ] Other____________________

6. How many years of teaching experience do you have? ______years

7. How many years have you taught bilingual/LEP/bicultural students (including this year)? ____________ years

8. Please characterize your current class(es):
   a. Grade level:________
   b. Language(s) of instruction: 1. Mostly Spanish 2. Mixed 3. Mostly English
   c. Subject:__________________________(Junior High only)

9. How would you characterize your effectiveness in teaching language arts to your current students?

Low 1	2	3	4	Extremely High 5

Project Effectiveness

10. Please rate the effectiveness of the project in each of the following areas:

	Poor		Adequate		Very Effective	NA
a) Communication with team members	1	2	3	4	5	6
b) Communication across teams	1	2	3	4	5	6
c) Motivating teachers to use technology in their classrooms	1	2	3	4	5	6
d) Making technology available in classrooms	1	2	3	4	5	6
e) Involving teachers in project decision making	1	2	3	4	5	6
f) Project management and organization	1	2	3	4	5	6
g) Project leadership	1	2	3	4	5	6
h) Project in-services	1	2	3	4	5	6
i) Work-study sessions	1	2	3	4	5	6
j) Operation of your Tech Center	1	2	3	4	5	6
k) Overall effectiveness of the project	1	2	3	4	5	6

Training

11. How effectively do you feel you have been trained by the program in the following areas?

	Poor		Adequate		Very effective	NA
a) Curriculum development	1	2	3	4	5	6
b) Use of equipment	1	2	3	4	5	6
c) Use of software	1	2	3	4	5	6
d) Language arts instruction	1	2	3	4	5	6
e) Integrating technology and language arts	1	2	3	4	5	6
f) Using technology with language minority students to meet your bilingual program's goals	1	2	3	4	5	6

12. How much follow-up and assistance has the project provided you in the following areas?

	None		Some		A Great Deal	NA
a) Use of technology in instruction	1	2	3	4	5	6
b) Planning and developing curriculum units and activities	1	2	3	4	5	6
c) Becoming familiar with and learning about technology	1	2	3	4	5	6
d) Training students in equipment usage	1	2	3	4	5	6
e) Integrating the use of technology with bilingual instruction	1	2	3	4	5	6

Use of Technology

13. Approximately how much has your class used the Tech Center this school year?
__________hours/week

14. On average, how much do you use technology as part of your regular classroom program (not including Tech Center time)? Please indicate which of these are permanently in your classroom:

		PERMANENTLY IN MY CLASSROOM
Video equipment	________hours/week	[ ]
Computer equipment	________hours/week	[ ]
Laser disc equipment	________hours/week	[ ]
Other:______________	________hours/week	[ ]

15. a. On average, how many *hours a month* do you spend doing the following project-related activities?
______hours a) Participating in project meetings and in-services
______hours b) Planning/developing instructional activities/curriculum units
______hours c) Becoming familiar with technology on your own
______hours d) Helping students in the use of the equipment during nonclass time
______hours e) Other (specify) ______________________________

b. About what percentage of this time is unreimbursed, nonschool time? ______%

16. How many times this school year have you shared your products and ideas with others?
a. At conferences__________
b. With non-MTS colleagues__________
c. Informal presentations__________

Effects of Project

17. To what extent has your involvement in the project affected your expectations for your students' achievement?

Greatly Lowered	Slightly Lowered	Has Not Affected	Slightly Increased	Greatly Increased
1	2	3	4	5

Please explain: ______________________________

____

____

____

____

18. How much of a difference (if any) has participating in the project had on your students' school-related attitudes and behaviors?

	None		Some		A Great Deal
a) Increased liking of school	1	2	3	4	5
b) Improved language arts skills	1	2	3	4	5
c) Improved confidence as a learner	1	2	3	4	5
d) Increased interest in technology	1	2	3	4	5
e) Improved student-teacher rapport	1	2	3	4	5
f) Increased participation in class	1	2	3	4	5
g) Improved student-student cooperation		1	2	3	45
h) Other (specify below):	1	2	3	4	5

____

19. Please rate the extent to which your involvement with the project has affected the following:

	None		Some		A Great Deal
a) Improved my overall teaching effectiveness	1	2	3	4	5
b) Improved my language arts instruction	1	2	3	4	5
c) Changed my perceptions about my students' learning abilities	1	2	3	4	5
d) Changed my instructional methods	1	2	3	4	5

Please explain these ratings:

a) ______________________________
b) ______________________________
c) ______________________________
d) ______________________________

20. Please rate the extent to which you agree or disagree with each of the following statements:

	Strongly Disagree	Disagree	Neutral	Agree	Strongly Agree
a) I am enthusiastic about participation in this project.	1	2	3	4	5
b) Administrators at my school are generally supportive of the project.	1	2	3	4	5
c) My principal provides strong support for my teaching.	1	2	3	4	5
d) I feel a lot of stress at work.	1	2	3	4	5
e) I am satisfied with my work environment.	1	2	3	4	5
f) I feel excited by my students' accomplishments.	1	2	3	4	5
g) The project is helping me develop professionally.	1	2	3	4	5
h) I am developing teacher training skills.	1	2	3	4	5

21. How satisfied are you with your students' progress in the following areas?

	Highly Satisfied		Neutral		Dissatisfied
Reading	5	4	3	2	1
Math	5	4	3	2	1
Writing	5	4	3	2	1
Science	5	4	3	2	1
Social Studies	5	4	3	2	1
Peer Relationships	5	4	3	2	1
Self-Confidence	5	4	3	2	1
Cultural Sensitivity	5	4	3	2	1
Motivation for Learning	5	4	3	2	1

22. Please share your impressions of the project's accomplishments and/or how it may be improved:

THANK YOU!!

Resource C: Sample Student Survey

The survey you are about to complete will ask you questions about you and about your school. This is NOT a test. There are no right or wrong answers. The survey will give you an opportunity to express how you feel about what happens in your classes and around school. That is why it is important to answer the questions as truthfully and as carefully as possible.

Do Not Write on These Pages

MARK YOUR ANSWERS ON THE ANSWER SHEET PROVIDED. You will notice that answers go from 1 to 5 or from 6 to 10. This does not matter. Simply choose the one answer that best fits your opinion for each question. MARK ONLY ONE LETTER ON THE ANSWER SHEET FOR EACH QUESTION. For example, if you chose answer 5 for question number 5, you would mark the answer sheet like this:

	1	2	3	4	5
5	○	○	○	○	●

Or, if you chose answer 9 for question number 6, you would mark the answer sheet like this:

	6	7	8	9	10
6	○	○	○	●	○

Remember, mark only one letter on the answer sheet for each question. If there are any words or questions you don't understand, please raise your hand and ask for help.

QUESTIONS ABOUT YOU

1. Sex:
    1. Male
    2. Female
2. In addition to English, what other languages are spoken in your home?
    1. None
    2. Spanish
    3. Vietnamese
    4. Chinese
    5. Other
3. Living situation:
    1. With two parents (includes stepparents)
    2. With one parent only (mother or father only)
    3. Guardian(s)/foster parents
    4. Alone or with friends
    5. Other
4. About how many hours a week do you usually spend working on a job during the school year?
    1. None: I am not employed during the school year.
    2. About 10 hours or less.
    3. About 15-20 hours
    4. About 20-30 hours
    5. More than 30 hours
5. How many hours do you watch television each day?
    1. None
    2. About 1 hour
    3. About 2-3 hours
    4. About 4-5 hours
    5. More than 5 hours

Choose the ONE answer that best completes each of the following sentences.

6. If I could do anything I want, I would like to
    1. quit school as soon as possible.
    2. finish high school
    3. go to trade/technical school or junior college
    4. go to a 4-year college or university
    5. don't know

7. I think my parents would like me to

   1. quit school as soon as possible
   2. finish high school
   3. go to trade/technical school or junior college
   4. go to a 4-year college or university
   5. don't know

8. Actually, I will probably

   1. quit school as soon as possible
   2. finish high school
   3. go to trade/technical school or junior college
   4. go to a 4-year college or university
   5. don't know

9. How comfortable do you feel about choosing a future career goal at this point in your life?

   1. Very uncomfortable
   2. Uncomfortable
   3. Neither uncomfortable nor comfortable
   4. Comfortable
   5. Very comfortable

The following sentences describe some of the ways in which people might think about themselves.Read each of the following sentences carefully and mark the number on the answer sheet that tells how much it is like you.

Look at the following practice sentence and mark the letter on the answer sheet that tells how much you agree or disagree with the sentence.

PRACTICE

	Strongly Agree	Mildly Agree	Not Sure	Mildly Disagree	Strongly Disagree
I am good at art	5	4	3	2	1

If you choose "Strongly Agree," you're saying that you are very good at art. If you choose "Mildly Agree," you're saying that you are OK at art. If you choose "Mildly Disagree," you're saying that you are not too good at art. If you choose "Strongly disagree," you're saying that you are very poor at art.

	Strongly Agree	Mildly Agree	Not Sure	Mildly Disagree	Strongly Disagree
10. I'm popular with kids my own age.	5	4	3	2	1
11. Kids usually follow my ideas.	5	4	3	2	1
12. Most people are better liked than I am.	5	4	3	2	1
13. It is hard for me to make friends.	5	4	3	2	1

14. I have no real friends.	5	4	3	2	1
15. I'm not doing as well as I'd like to in school.	5	4	3	2	1
16. I am a good reader.	5	4	3	2	1
17. I'm proud of my school work.	5	4	3	2	1
18. I'm good at math.	5	4	3	2	1
19. I'm doing the best work that I can.	5	4	3	2	1
20. I am able to do schoolwork at least as well as other students.	5	4	3	2	1
21. My grades are not good enough.	5	4	3	2	1
22. I'm always making mistakes in my schoolwork.	5	4	3	2	1
23. I am a good writer.	5	4	3	2	1

QUESTIONS ABOUT YOUR SCHOOL LIFE

How much do the following words describe most of the teachers at this school?

	Very Much	Pretty Much	Some-what	Only a Little Bit	Not at All
24. Friendly	5	4	3	2	1
25. Helpful	5	4	3	2	1
26. Have high hopes for us	5	4	3	2	1
27. Talk to us	5	4	3	2	1
28. Let us talk to them	5	4	3	2	1
29. Care about us	5	4	3	2	1
30. Do a good job	5	4	3	2	1

How much do the following words describe how you feel about most of the students at this school?

	Very Much	Pretty Much	Some-what	Only a Little Bit	Not at All
31. Friendly	5	4	3	2	1
32. Helpful	5	4	3	2	1
33. Have high hopes	5	4	3	2	1
34. Smart	5	4	3	2	1
35. Talk to each other	5	4	3	2	1
36. Care about each other	5	4	3	2	1
37. Competitive	5	4	3	2	1

38. The most popular students in this school are (choose only one answer):
    1. Athletes
    2. Smart students
    3. Members of student government
    4. Good-looking students
    5. Wealthy students

Indicate whether or not you participate in the following activities at school. (Anser yes or no for each of the following.)

	Yes	No
39. I participate in sports teams/drill team/flags/cheerleading	1	2
40. I participate in student government	1	2
41. I participate in music, band, drama, or other arts	1	2
42. I participate in honor society	1	2
43. I participate in school clubs/community service activities	1	2

Below is a list of things that may be problems at this school. How much do you think each is a problem at this school?

	Not a Problem	Minor Problem	Major Problem
44. Student misbehavior (fighting, stealing, gangs, truancy, etc.)	1	2	3
45. Poor courses or not enough different subjects offered	1	2	3
46. Prejudice/racial conflict	1	2	3
47. Drugs	1	2	3
48. Alcohol	1	2	3
49. Poor teachers or teaching	1	2	3
50. School too large/classes overcrowded	1	2	3
51. Teachers don't discipline students	1	2	3
52. Poor or not enough buildings, equipment, or materials	1	2	3
53. The principal and other people in the office who run the school	1	2	3
54. Poor student attitudes (poor school spirit, don't want to learn)	1	2	3
55. Too many rules and regulations	1	2	3
56. How the school is organized (class schedules, not enough time for lunch, passing periods, etc.)	1	2	3

ISSUES AND PROBLEMS

Read each one of the following sentences carefully and choose the letter that tells how much you agree or disagree with what it says. CHOOSE ONLY ONE NUMBER for each sentence. Please raise your hand if you have any questions.

	Strongly Agree	Mildly Agree	Not Sure	Mildly Disagree	Strongly Disagree
57. I think students of different races or colors should go to school together.	5	4	3	2	1
58. There are places at this school where I don't go because I am afraid of other students.	5	4	3	2	1
59. I do not have enough time to do my schoolwork.	5	4	3	2	1
60. Some of the things teachers want me to learn are just too hard.	5	4	3	2	1
61. If I had my choice, I would go to a different school.	5	4	3	2	1

62. There are things I want to learn about that this school doesn't teach.	5	4	3	2	1
63. It's not safe to walk to and from school alone.	5	4	3	2	1
64. I have trouble reading the books and materials in my classes.	5	4	3	2	1
65. The grades or marks I get help me to learn better.	5	4	3	2	1
66. I like school.	5	4	3	2	1
67. The grades or marks I get in class have nothing to do with what I really know.	5	4	3	2	1
68. I have to learn things without really knowing why.	5	4	3	2	1
69. Parents should have a say in what is taught at school.	5	4	3	2	1
70. It is easy for me to get help from a counselor when planning my school program.	5	4	3	2	1
71. We are not given enough freedom in choosing our classes.	5	4	3	2	1
72. We are not given enough freedom in choosing our teachers.	5	4	3	2	1
73. If I have a personal problem, it would be easy for me to get help from a counselor.	5	4	3	2	1
74. If you don't want to go to college, this school doesn't think you're very important.	5	4	3	2	1
75. Students should have a say in what is taught at this school.	5	4	3	2	1
76. A person is foolish to keep going to school if he/she can get a job.	5	4	3	2	1
77. If I need help planning for a career, it would be easy for me to get help from a counselor.	5	4	3	2	1
78. I like the way the school looks.	5	4	3	2	1
79. It is easy to get books from the school library.	5	4	3	2	1
80. Things in the school library are useful to me.	5	4	3	2	1
81. Materials in the Career Guidance Center (CGC) are useful to me.	5	4	3	2	1

QUESTIONS ABOUT TEACHING, LEARNING, AND CLASSROOM WORK

All schools teach pretty much the same things, but they may think some things are more important than others.

82. Which ONE of these does this school think is the most important thing for students? (Choose only one.)
    1. To work well with other people.
    2. To learn the basic skills in reading, writing, arithmetic, and other subjects.
    3. To become a better person.
    4. To get a good job.

83. If you had to choose only the ONE most important thing for you, which would it be? (Choose only one.)
    1. To work well with other people.
    2. To learn the basic skills in reading, writing, arithmetic, and other subjects.
    3. To become a better person.
    4. To get a good job.

In general, how do you like the following subjects?

	Like Very Much	Like Somewhat	Undecided	Dislike Somewhat	Dislike Very Much
84. English	5	4	3	2	1
85. Mathematics	5	4	3	2	1
86. Social Studies (history, geography, government, etc.)	5	4	3	2	1
87. Science	5	4	3	2	1
88. Computer Education	5	4	3	2	1
89. The Arts (art, crafts, music, drama, dance, creative writing, filmmaking, photography)	5	4	3	2	1
90. Foreign Language	5	4	3	2	1
91. Vocational/Career Education (shop, business education, home economics, etc.)	5	4	3	2	1
92. Physical education	5	4	3	2	1

93. How many hours of homework do you do each day?
    1. None
    2. About 1 hour
    3. About 2-3 hours
    4. About 4-5 hours
    5. More than 5 hours

94. In general how often do you do your homework?
    1. All of the time
    2. Most of the time
    3. Sometimes
    4. Seldom
    5. Never
95. How soon do teachers usually return your work?
    1. The next day
    2. 2 days later
    3. 3 days later
    4. 4 days later
    5. 5 days later or more
96. When you make mistakes in your work, how often do teachers tell you how to do it corretly?
    1. All of the time
    2. Most of the time
    3. Only sometimes
    4. Seldom
    5. Never
97. How often do your parents or other family members help you with your schoolwork?
    1. All of the time
    2. Most of the time
    3. Only sometimes
    4. Seldom
    5. Never

Listed below are four ways students can work in a classroom. Choose the number on the answer sheet that tells how much you like or would like to work in each way, even if you don't do so now.

	Like Very Much	Like Somewhat	Undecided	Dislike Somewhat	Dislike Very Much
98. Alone by myself	5	4	3	2	1
99. With the whole class	5	4	3	2	1
100. With a small group of students who know as much as I do	5	4	3	2	1
101. With a small group of students, some who know less, some who know as much, and some who know more than I do	5	4	3	2	1

Listed below are some things that might be used in a class. Choose the number on the answer sheet that tells how much you like or would like to use each thing, even if you don't use it in a classroom.

	Like Very Much	Like Somewhat	Unde-cided	Dislike Somewhat	Dislike Very Much
102. Textbooks	5	4	3	2	1
103. Other books	5	4	3	2	1
104. Worksheets	5	4	3	2	1
105. Films, filmstrips, or slides	5	4	3	2	1
106. Games or simulations	5	4	3	2	1
107. Newspapers or magazines	5	4	3	2	1
108. Tape recordings or records	5	4	3	2	1
109. Television/video	5	4	3	2	1
110. Calculators	5	4	3	2	1
111. Globes, maps, and charts	5	4	3	2	1
112. Animals and plants	5	4	3	2	1
113. Lab equipment and material	5	4	3	2	1
114. Computers	5	4	3	2	1

Listed below are some things that you might do in a class. Choose the number on the answer sheet that tells how much you like or would like to do each thing, even if you don't do it in class.

	Like Very Much	Like Somewhat	Unde-cided	Dislike Somewhat	Dislike Very Much
115. Listen to the teacher	5	4	3	2	1
116. Go on field trips	5	4	3	2	1
117. Do research and write reports, stories, or poems	5	4	3	2	1
118. Listen to student reports	5	4	3	2	1
119. Listen to speakers who come to class	5	4	3	2	1
120. Have class discussions	5	4	3	2	1
121. Build or draw things	5	4	3	2	1
122. Do problems or write answers to questions	5	4	3	2	1
123. Take tests or quizzes	5	4	3	2	1
124. Make films or recordings	5	4	3	2	1
125. Act things out	5	4	3	2	1
126. Read for fun or interest	5	4	3	2	1
127. Read for information	5	4	3	2	1
128. Interview people	5	4	3	2	1
129. Do projects or experiments that are already planned	5	4	3	2	1
130. Do projects or experiments that I plan	5	4	3	2	1

Please indicate how important each of the following items was in your choice of classes here at Royal High School.

	Very Important	Important	Not Sure	Not Important	Very Un-important
131. Taking classes from teachers I like	5	4	3	2	1
132. Being in the same classes as my friends	5	4	3	2	1
133. Completing graduation requirements	5	4	3	2	1
134. Learning skills for a future job	5	4	3	2	1
135. Taking classes that will help me be a better person	5	4	3	2	1
136. Being challenged by taking hard subjects	5	4	3	2	1
137. Taking classes that will prepare me for the future	5	4	3	2	1
138. Getting a wide variety of classes	5	4	3	2	1
139. Preparing for college	5	4	3	2	1
140. Taking classes that require little work	5	4	3	2	1
141. Avoiding subjects I don't like	5	4	3	2	1
142. Taking classes that are popular	5	4	3	2	1
143. Taking classes my parent(s) consider important	5	4	3	2	1
144. Taking classes where I can get good grades	5	4	3	2	1

QUESTIONS ABOUT THE LEARNING RESOURCE CENTER (LRC)

145. Have you heard of the Learning Resource Center?

    1. Yes
    2. No

146. If yes, how often have you gone with your classes to the Learning Resource Center?

    1. Never
    2. Only once or twice
    3. About once or twice an month
    4. About once or twice a week
    5. Almost every day

147. How often have you gone to the Learning Resource Center by yourself?

    1. Never
    2. Only once or twice
    3. About once or twice an month
    4. About once or twice a week
    5. Almost every day

If you have ever used the Learning Resource Center, have you used any of these services? (Answer yes or no for each of the following.)

	Yes	No
148. Diagnostic testing for reading and math problems	1	2
149. Entry testing for proper class placement	1	2
150. Assistance with assignments from classroom teacher	1	2
151. Work on tasks assigned by the Learning Resource Center	1	2
152. After-school seminars	1	2
153. Study hall	1	2
154. SAT preparation	1	2
155. Proficiency test preparation	1	2
156. Use the computer	1	2
157. Study skills	1	2
158. Language laboratory	1	2
159. Assistance in researching or typing papers	1	2
160. Use the typewriter	1	2
161. Receive individual tutoring	1	2
162. Develop library/research skills	1	2
163. Develop reading skills	1	2
164. Develop writing skills	1	2
165. Develop math skills	1	2
166. Develop listening skills	1	2
167. Develop test taking skills	1	2
168. Have you received credit for Writing I through the Learning Resource Center?	1	2
169. Have you received credit for Developmental Reading through the Learning Resource Center?	1	2

	Strongly Agree	Mildly Agree	Not Sure	Mildly Disagree	Strongly Disagree
170. The Learning Resource Center is helping students at Royal.	5	4	3	2	1
171. Most students know about the resources available in the Learning Resource Center.	5	4	3	2	1
172. I have been helped by the services of the Learning Resource Center.	5	4	3	2	1
173. I am comfortable about using the services of the Learning Resource Center.	5	4	3	2	1
174. My work in the Learning Resource Center has helped me in my courses.	5	4	3	2	1
175. My work in the Learning Resource Center has made me feel more secure about my ability to do the work assigned by my teachers.	5	4	3	2	1

QUESTIONS ABOUT THE CAREER MAGNET SCHOOL

	Strongly Agree	Mildly Agree	Not Sure	Mildly Disagree	Strongly Disagree
176. I understand what the Career Magnet School program is trying to do.	5	4	3	2	1
177. I would like more information about the Career Magnet Schools.	5	4	3	2	1

Resource D: Worksheets

Worksheet 1.1
Evaluation Focus and Priority Questions

	Priority Rating			
Questions	*Low*	*Medium*	*High*	*Required*
Outcomes:				
Curriculum:				
Instruction:				
Staff:				
Parents and Community:				

Worksheet 2.1

Tracking Strategies

Evaluation Questions	1. 2. 3. 4. 5. 6.		
Questions	*Evidence of Progress*	*Source of Information (Instruments)*	*Standards of Success*

Worksheet 3.1
Instrument Blueprints

Instrument	*Questions Asked*
Portfolios	
Parent Questionnaire	
Student Questionnaire	
Faculty Interviews	
Standardized Nationally Normed	
State Assessment	
Competency	
Other	

Worksheet 3.2
Data Collection Management Plan

Task by Instrument	*Person Responsible*	*Sampling*	*Sept.*	*Oct.*	*Nov.*	*Dec.*	*Jan.*	*Feb.*	*Mar.*	*Apr.*	*May*
Instrument: Math Portfolios Select group to develop/choose Develop tasks and criteria Produce Distribute Administer Score Analyze and interpret											
Instrument: Math Chapter Tests Select group to develop/choose Develop tasks and criteria Produce Distribute Administer Score Analyze and interpret											
Instrument: State Assessment Select group to develop/choose Develop tasks and criteria Produce Distribute Administer Score Analyze and interpret											
Instrument: ITBS Select group to develop/choose Develop tasks and criteria Produce Distribute Administer Score Analyze and interpret											

Worksheet 4.1
Summarizing Data

Instrument	*Score Selected*	*Summary Method*
Questionnaire/Survey		
Nationally Normed Test		
Selected Response Curriculum-Related Tests		
Performance Tests		
Interviews (open-ended responses)		
Archival Information		

Worksheet 5.1
Data Analysis for Specific Evaluation Questions

Question: In what areas are we in need of improvement?

Instrument	*Score Used*	*Analysis*

Question: How well are we implementing a process-based approach to writing?

Instrument	*Score Used*	*Analysis*

Question: Is student writing improving?

Instrument	*Score Used*	*Analysis*

Question: Do students feel positive about the writing program?

Instrument	*Score Used*	*Analysis*

Worksheet 6.1

Communicate and Act on Findings

		Report Format		
Audiences	***Key Concern(s)***	***Formal***	***Informal***	***Date***
Teachers:				
Students:				
Parents:				
School Board:				
Community:				
District/Other Administrators:				
Other:				

Key for entering report format:
H = Handouts: tables, sample items/performance tasks, score summaries, and so on
N = Newsletter: school, district, PTA
O = Oral, informal report: faculty meetings, district meetings
P = Presentation: formal, with invited audience, agenda, overheads, and so on
T = Technical report: formal, written report following format of research report

Resource E: Sample Report Card

Report to Parents

Brighton School

727 S. Brighton Ave.
Covina, CA 91723

Mrs. Georgia Florentine, Principal — November 1991

School Profile

Brighton School is one of twelve K-6 schools in the Covina-Valley Unified School District. The enrollment as of October 1, 1991 was 629 students. The ethnic makeup of the school is indicated on the following chart:

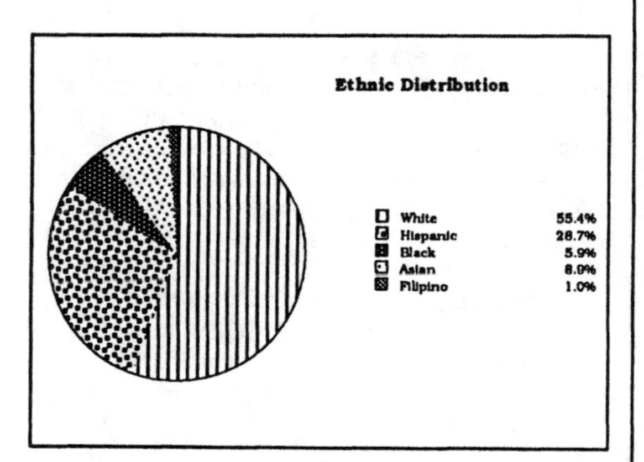

Note: Because of rounding, the percentages may not total to exactly 100%.

Brighton School was built in 1952. Since 1987 , 5 new relocatables have increased the number of classrooms to 23. These additions allow us to accommodate the growth in student population in our community.

A California Compact with the South Hills Kiwanis Club was recently formed to set up a buddy tutoring program. In addition, enrichment for Brighton students is provided by a partnership with the local Carl's Jr.

Instructional and Support Staff

Brighton's teaching staff includes 22 regular education teachers, 1 special education teacher, instrumental/choral/classroom music teachers and 1 Title VII resource teacher. All teachers have assignments within their credential authorization.

Additional personnel include the school principal, secretary, office clerk, custodian, janitor, food services staff, and 17 instructional aides and a home school assistant.

In addition, psychologists, nurses, language and speech specialists, an audiologist, and an adapted P.E. specialist are available to provide support in meeting the academic, personal, and emotional needs of our students. Child abuse prevention programs and a crisis response team are also in place.

Advanced degrees are held by 60% of the certificated staff.

Quality of Instruction and Leadership

All students are expected to develop effective oral and written communication skills, solve mathematical problems and think logically. Teachers use instructional strategies that promote active involvement of all students and administrators serve as instructional leaders. A continuous effort is made to ensure that all students regardless of special need, e.g., limited English speaking, special education, gifted, have access to the core curriculum.

The quality of the school's instructional program is assessed every 4 years using the State Consolidated Program Review . During the last review, the visiting committee stated that the strengths of the school were:

- Enthusiastic, positive learning environment.
- Strong commitment to academic excellence.

Academic Performance

Because of statewide cutbacks within California Assessment Program during the 1990-91 school year, the CAP exams were not administered. The following information is based on the latest CAP scores. Third and sixth graders at Brighton School took the California Assessment Program (CAP) exam in May of 1990. The exam uses a scale from 100 to 400, with the statewide average set at 250 the first year the test was administered. In May 1990, third graders scored 310 in reading, 307 in written language, and 320 in mathematics. The sixth graders scored 328 in reading, 299 in written language, and 330 in mathematics. The following graphs show three-year comparisons of scores:

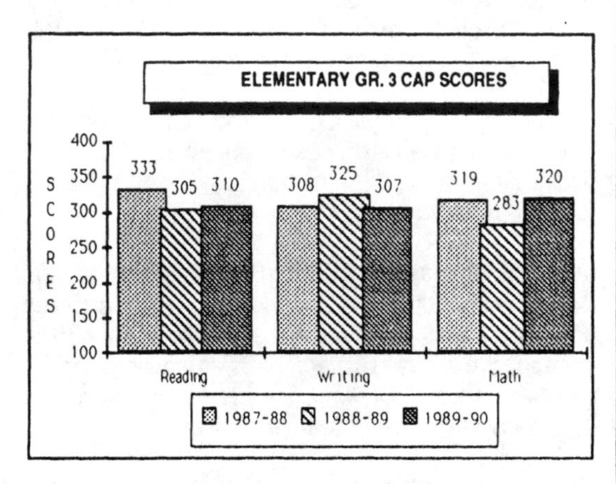

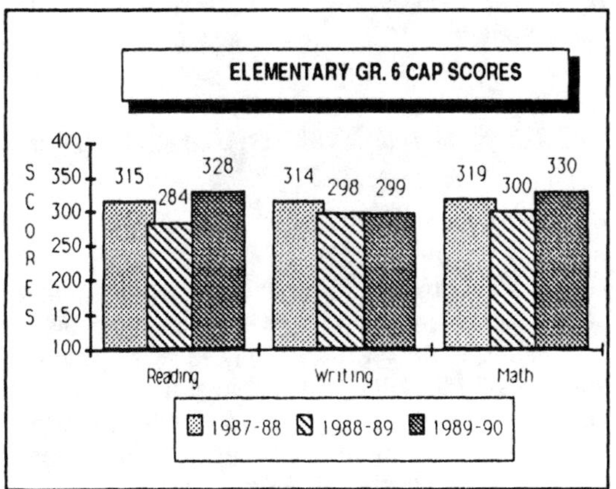

Student Attendance

During the 1990-91 school year, an average of 94.0% of all students at Brighton School were in attendance. It is estimated that 1% of student attendance days were generated by students who did not attend full minimum instructional days because of unexcused absences. Parents are encouraged to have their sons and daughters attend every day during the school year. Success in school depends on the ability to acquire specific skills and knowledge in all classes every day of the year.

Class Size

California ranks as one of the highest in the nation in the number of students per teacher. As of October 1, 1991 Brighton's average class size was 28.6 students per teacher. The average class size for K-3 was 27.8 and 4-6 was 29.6 students per teacher. Class enrollment is balanced to keep class size as low as possible.

Substitute Teachers

When teachers are absent, it is the District's goal to employ the highest quality substitutes available. Because there is a general shortage of substitute teachers throughout California, the District maintains a competitive substitute salary rate and has an ongoing recruitment program to employ qualified substitute teachers. All substitute teachers hold a valid California teaching credential based upon a bachelor's degree and have passed the California Basic Educational Skills Test (CBEST) when that is a requirement; many of them, including those who have retired from Covina-Valley, have regular teaching experience.

District Expenditure

The C-VUSD is spending an average of $4,107 per student for all educational services including salaries, instructional materials, maintenance, transportation, and capital expenses.

In addition, our school receives specialized funds for the following programs:

- Chapter 1
- Chapter 2
- Gifted and Talented Education (GATE)
- Limited English Proficient (LEP)
- School Improvement (SI)
- Title VII
- Special Education

- High teacher involvement in staff development.
- Leadership and support from many onsite Mentor teachers.
- Special needs services by GATE, LEP, RSP, Speech and Chapter 1.

Climate for Learning

Brighton's goal is to provide a positive climate for learning in order to assure student achievement, enhance self-esteem, and develop positive social behavior. To reach this goal, Brighton School has the following opportunities for student participation and recognition:

- Principal's Awards
- Monthly Citizenship Assemblies
- Performing Arts
- Perfect Attendance Awards
- Presidential Academic Fitness Awards

Students are expected to maintain appropriate behavior at all times because classroom disruptions interfere with learning. School rules and procedures are distributed and discussed on a regular basis. Parent support in recognizing their children for positive efforts in this area benefits the educational program.

Textbooks/Instructional Materials

Covina-Valley USD follows a cycle for adoption of State approved textbooks. Each major curricular area is reviewed every seven years by representative teacher committees and modified as necessary. Appropriate textbooks and other instructional materials are purchased to support the program.

A math program was implemented with the purchase of a new textbook series in 1988. Core literature books were purchased and are now being used in the classroom. In 1990-91, a new language arts program stressing quality literature and frequent writing was implemented and new material was purchased. This year a new social science program has been implemented and new materials purchased.

The library contains 6,500 volumes and is staffed by an instructional aide. There are 32 computers, distributed throughout the school in individual classrooms. The resource room contains a wide variety of supplemental materials. A valuable collection of classroom sets of literature books is also available for checkout. LEP and Chapter 1 students utilize this facility daily.

Curriculum Improvement and Training

Each major subject area is reviewed and revised every seven years. After curriculum is revised and new courses of study or course descriptions are written, appropriate instructional materials are selected and staff in-service programs designed. New programs are developed based on the latest research in curriculum and instruction and State frameworks.

Many in-service opportunities are available for teachers and administrators during school, after school and during the summer. Teachers, administrators, and support staff receive training at the school, the District Office or attend workshops or conferences throughout Southern California. Presenters are often Covina-Valley Unified School District teachers, many working as Mentor Teachers with special projects such as Math Manipulatives, Cooperative Learning, The Writing Process, The Use of Literature in the Classroom and Learning Styles. Most in-service opportunities are directly related to new directions in the curricular program and new teaching strategies.

New teachers receive training before their first teaching day and continual support from many sources including Mentor teachers.

Teacher Evaluation and Professional Improvement

The purpose of the teacher evaluation process is to improve instruction. While all teachers are observed and evaluated informally on an ongoing basis as needed, under the law nontenured teachers are formally evaluated in writing every year and tenured teachers at least every other year. Examples of evaluation areas are instructional methodology, suitable learning environment, and classroom management. Teachers and the principal receive appropriate training in these areas.

State law requires that comparative salary and budget information — which is taken from documents available to the general public — be displayed in each school's Report to Parents:

Salary Categories (1989-90)		Covina-Valley's Average		Comparison — State Average Districts over 1,500 ADA *	Comparison — State Average Districts from 10,001 - 25,000 ADA *		
Teachers		Annual Salary	Daily Pay	Annual Salary	Annual Salary	Daily Pay	Annual Salary Range
	Beginning	$24,970	$136	$23,779	$24,273	$131	$20,265-$29,000
	Mid-range	$43,150	$235	$36,952	$37,987	$205	$32,218-$43,241
	Highest	$47,440	$258	$45,284	$47,352	$256	$41,046-$53,939
School Administrators (average)		$64,027	$291	$57,284	$59,855	$280	$40,363-$68,670
Superintendents		$84,648	$376	$82,324	$87,683	$391	$60,895-$114,784
Budget Percentages (1989-90)							
For Teachers' Salaries		41.37%		44.01%	44.25%		38.79%-48.33%
For Administrative Salaries		4.46%		5.69%	5.82%		4.73%-8.72%

* ADA means Average Daily Attendance

Safety

As part of the school's commitment to a safe and orderly campus, Brighton School has an earthquake/disaster preparedness plan and conducts regular fire and emergency drills.

Safety concerns, when identified by the District safety committee or the school staff, are referred to the District Maintenance Department for correction.

Index

9 780803 960244